Measuring for Results

Measuring for Results

The Dimensions of
Public Library Effectiveness

Joseph R. Matthews

LIBRARIES
UNLIMITED
A Member of the Greenwood Publishing Group
Westport, Connecticut • London

Library of Congress Cataloging in-Publication Data

Matthews, Joseph R.
  Measuring for results : the dimensions of public library effectiveness / Joseph R. Matthews
    p. cm.
  Includes bibliographical references and index.
  ISBN 1–59158–100–1 (alk. paper)
    1. Public libraries—Evaluation. 2. Public libraries—United States—Evaluation. 3. Organizational effectiveness—Measurement. I. Title.
  Z678.85.M38 2004
  027.6—dc22   2003060764

British Library Cataloguing in Publication Data is available.

Library of Congress Catalog Card Number: 2003060764
ISBN: 1–59158–100–1

First published in 2004

Libraries Unlimited, Inc., 88 Post Road West, Westport, CT 06881
A Member of the Greenwood Publishing Group, Inc.
www.lu.com

Printed in the United States of America

The paper used in this book complies with the Permanent Paper Standard issued by the National Information Standards Organization (Z39.48–1984).

10 9 8 7 6 5 4 3 2 1

To Martha

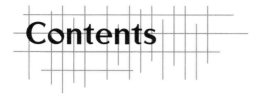

Contents

Acknowledgments

Early in life I was fortunate to acquire the reading bug and thus have enjoyed many pleasurable hours reading both fiction and nonfiction. I also was introduced to libraries as a child and acquired the "library habit," which expanded my horizons considerably. When I first started attending the American Library Association annual meetings, I was fortunate to develop a friendship with Kevin Hegarty, who for many years was the director of the Tacoma Public Library. It was Kevin who first introduced to me the importance of performance measures in public libraries.

I am particularly indebted to a number of people who took the time to carefully read and comment on my first draft and thereby made this book better, including: Jim Scheppke, Oregon State Librarian; Keith Curry Lance, director of Research at the Colorado State Library; and Ken Dowlin, formerly director of the San Francisco Public Library and now professor at the School of Library & Information Science at San Jose State University. Their substantive comments and suggestions improved the clarity of the material presented in this book. Any errors, faults, and limitations of this work are obviously mine and should not reflect upon them.

I am also grateful to that wonderful service afforded to library users called interlibrary loan (ILL). A great many libraries provided photocopies and loaned books so that I could become better informed about the topic of performance measures in public libraries. In particular I should note the terrific service provided by the ILL staff at San Jose State University and California State University, San Marcos libraries. It is much appreciated!

I would also like to acknowledge the staff at Libraries Unlimited for their assistance in producing this book, including Martin Dillon, Emma Bailey, and Ron Maas.

Joe Matthews
Carlsbad, CA

xi

Chapter

Introduction

Libraries are really one of the greatest gifts that the American people have ever given themselves. They're a gift for all of us—no restrictions of age or gender or class or interest.—Barbara Bush[1]

The importance of determining and communicating the value of public library services to various stakeholders is critical so that continued funding and support of the libraries will be assured. Historically, librarians have relied on the perceived "value or goodness" of the public library as a means to garnering financial support for the library. One of the manifestations of this support is the fact that roughly 75 percent of the elections held over the last 10 years to fund new library construction or expand the tax base for the library's annual operating budget have been approved by voters across the United States.

However, it is now becoming apparent that public libraries must be able to demonstrate, using an acceptable methodology, the economic value of the library and its services to individuals, businesses, and the surrounding local community. Using one or even several approaches, it is possible to estimate the benefits and impacts of the public library so that a return on investment (ROI) calculation can be performed.

Attempting to assess the impact or outcomes of the services provided by a public library is difficult in the best of circumstances since, in most cases, the output measures are only indirect indicators of the value received. For example, in a public library setting, if someone borrows a book on resume writing, job-interviewing skills, and so forth and subsequently receives an offer for employment, the borrowing and use of the library materials did not directly lead to the job. The library materials no doubt assisted the individual in receiving the job offer, but they were not sole reason for that offer and thus it is almost impossible to determine the economic impact that these materials had.

As public agencies, public libraries have always had to demonstrate accountability and prudent fiscal management to ensure the continuing trust of the public and approval of their future funding requests. Historically, public libraries have relied on a few basic approaches to demonstrate value: accessibility, user satisfaction, response times, and output indicators that measure use of the library and its services. In addition, in most cases public libraries have focused on providing statistics about specific library services and their use rather than attempting to evaluate the total library.

A public library is provided with a set of *resources*. Those resources are organized and managed so that they have the *capability* to provide a set of services. The patrons or users of the library then utilize these capabilities or services. Once utilized, the services have a positive, beneficial *impact or effect* on the individual and, indirectly, on the community or society at large. The relationship among these variables, first articulated by R. H. Orr, is shown in Figure 1.1.

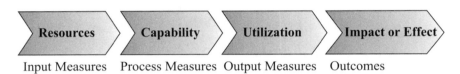

Figure 1.1. General Evaluation Model. Adapted from R. H. Orr. Progress in Documentation—Measuring the Goodness of Library Services: A General Framework for Considering Quantitative Measures. *Journal of Documentation*, **29 (3), September 1973, 315–32.**

The *input measures* are associated with the resources or inputs that have been allocated to the library. These input measures are also the easiest to gather and historically have been reported to state libraries on an annual basis. Examples of input measures are the annual budget, size of the collection, number of professional staff, and hours open each week. The American Library Association and the Public Library Association have a history of focusing on developing input measures and establishing library standards based on these input measures.[2] A number of state libraries and state library associations used these input measures as a basis for establishing library standards within their states.

Process measures have to do with the activities that transform resources into services offered by the library and as such are internally directed. Typically, process measures will quantify the cost or time to perform a specific task or activity. For example, the cost to order an item, the cost to receive a journal title, and the time it takes to receive and place an item on the shelf for clients to use are all examples of process measures. Essentially process measures are about efficiency. Efficiency answers the question: "Are we doing *things* right?"

Output measures indicate the degree to which the library and its services are being utilized. Typically, output measures are counts that measure volume of activity. Thus, annual circulation, number of reference questions answered, and number of people entering the library are examples of output measures. Librarians have used output measures as measures of goodness –the more the library's collection and its services were being used, the better! In the late 1980s and 1990s, the Public Library Association, a part of the American Library Association, developed a new set of initiatives focused on output measures.[3]

Sometimes a library will use a set of performance measures to compare its performance with the same measures in other similar libraries. In other cases, a group of similar libraries is divided into two groups: those within and those outside the state. The thrust of the emphasis on output measures was to encourage a public library to set goals and objectives relevant to their own community and to measure progress toward achieving those objectives. These output measures were used by some states to establish public library standards.

Outcome measures indicate the impact or effects of the public library and its information services on a specific individual and the surrounding community. Outcome measures for a public library are difficult to assess, and efforts to identify these outputs have been attempted in very few libraries.

Several words have been used to characterize the "effects" achieved by public library services:

- *impact*, the effect or influence of one person, thing, action, or service on another;

- *outcome*, the consequence, practical result, or effect of an event or activity;

- *value*, the importance of something, the perception of actual or potential benefit; and

- *benefit*, the helpful or useful effect that a thing or service has.[4]

It is possible to divide the potential beneficial outcomes or impacts of a public library into two broad groups, economic and social, as shown in Figure 1.2 (page 4). An economic benefit is an impact or outcome that can be quantified in some way. Social and community benefits cannot be quantified but still provide a positive impact and thus should be acknowledged. In some cases, the literature will refer to a tangible benefit, which is essentially an economic benefit, whereas an intangible benefit is similar to a social benefit. Potential measures of possible economic and social benefits are discussed in later chapters of this book.

Single Measure

A few efforts have been made to establish a single measure that would assess a library. Daniel O'Connor developed "The Library Quotient" by converting eight ratio scores, such as circulation per capita and reference questions per capita, using data from over 300 New Jersey public libraries.[5] It was suggested that using a library quotient score would make it possible to compare and contrast a library for evaluation and planning purposes. The use of the library quotient did not catch on.

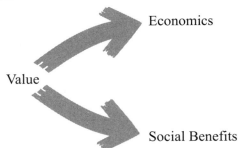

Economics

Value

Social Benefits

Figure 1.2. Possible Public Library Benefits

More recently, Thomas J. Hennen, a librarian, has developed Hennen's American Public Library Ratings (or HAPLR Index).[6] Using data collected annually through the Federal-State Cooperative System for public library data (FSCS), the HAPLR Index includes 15 weighted factors. The focus is on circulation, staffing, materials, reference service, and funding levels. (Data on audio and video collections and interlibrary loan, as well as measures of electronic database use or Internet service, are not included, since these data are not collected by the FSCS.)

The HAPLR Index has not been without its critics! For example, Jim Scheppke has noted that it is heavily weighted toward circulation-related statistics, some measures are redundant, and the index fails to address how these particular measures are, by definition, the "best" or "excellence." In addition, the index fails to consider such important aspects of a public library as the number of hours the library is open, how comfortable and spacious the library building is, the number of computers available, and whether the collection contains recently published books and other materials.[7] The use of an index, such as the HAPLR Index, only attempts to measure how "good" a library is and does not focus on the more important question: "Do public library services have a 'good' impact or benefit on the individual and the community?"

In addition, Keith Lance and Marti Cox attacked the HALPR Index on methodological grounds and suggested that developing a valid index can't be done given the current body of statistical data and is pointless as a basis of comparison since each library's service area and governance make comparisons pointless. Ultimately, each public library should be judged using criteria that will have relevance and meaning to local officials.[8]

Others have suggested that it would be possible to develop a total services index (TSI) that would add up the total annual circulation plus total in-library use of materials plus total reference questions answered plus total attendance at library events plus total number of individuals that log on to the library's Web site to gain access to electronic resources. Although such a TSI number would obviously be large, and perhaps impressive, it would not really convey the value of the public library.

Barry McIntyre has suggested developing an excellence index (E-Index) by using a standard score for each criterion and then adding the results to create a cumulative score. The E-Index is composed of six measures: collection size per capita, current rate of acquisitions, collection discards per capita, number of staff per 1,000 population, collection turnover rate, and circulation per capita.[9] Although there is a strong correlation between libraries' E-Index scores and their expenditures per capita, this only accounted for 43 percent of the variations in scores. Other factors such as location of the library facility and leadership also had an impact. McIntyre suggested using the E-Index as a basis for comparing an individual library to other libraries.

Culture of Assessment

The majority of public libraries simply collect statistics, as required by the state library or by tradition. Periodically one or more additional statistics—another name for performance measures—will be added to the mix. But very few libraries actually have given thought to how to employ a set of performance measures to manage and improve the services provided by the local public library. Thus, very few public libraries have what Larry White calls a "culture of assessment." White explored the use and impact of performance measures in Florida public libraries in his dissertation.[10] He found that although a wide variety of performance measures are used by public libraries, the measures are misaligned with stakeholder and organizational strategic needs, there are a lot of data that, although collected, are never used, and there are concerns about the accuracy of some of the data that are gathered.

In addition, the vast majority of performance measures and statistics collected by public libraries reflect past performance, often called "lagging indicators." The library profession has not yet identified a theory or generated an understanding concerning the relationships of inputs to outputs and outcomes. That is, there are very few, if any, "leading" performance measures that can be monitored that will accurately predict the outputs and/or outcomes of a public library 12 to 18 months later. This lack of understanding means that there can be no articulation of a cause-and-effect relationship between various types of public library performance measures.

An example might help improve the understanding of the cause-and-effect relationships. Sears, the large retailer, discovered that if it increased its investment in training employees, employee satisfaction would increase. Increased employee satisfaction led to increased customer satisfaction that, in turn, led to higher customer expenditures and greater profits for Sears.[11] In short, Sears discovered a cause-and-effect relationship between different types of performance measures. Investment in training is a leading indicator, whereas higher levels of customer satisfaction and profits for Sears are lagging indicators. That is, it takes some time from providing the training until the marketplace notices and starts spending more at Sears.

For libraries that move to a culture of assessment, the collection and analysis of data (performance measures) allow a library to make changes, monitor progress toward reaching its goals, significantly improve efficiency, and improve customer satisfaction.[12] And while there are a host of tools that can be used to complement the data collected through the use of performance measures, it is crucial to focus on change that will lead to improvements in effectiveness (Are we doing the right things?) rather than solely focusing on efficiency. (Are we doings things right? The "things" the library is providing may be appropriate and meet the needs of users or may, in fact, be the "wrong" things.)

Developing the cause-and-effect relationships among a variety of performance measures will allow librarians to develop a theory of public library service that can be improved over the course of time. For example, the vast majority of public libraries with branches assess the performance of each branch library by comparing annual circulation with prior year circulation figures. Yet the circulation figures—a one-dimensional output measure—clearly do not reflect the actual performance of a branch library and all of its services and contribution to its neighborhood. Issues such as the geographical boundaries of its catchment area, demographic characteristics of its population, hours open, size of its collection, quality of staff, range of services offered, location of the facility, ready availability of parking, and a host of other factors will affect the use of the local library. Yet these factors have not been identified in a consistent manner such that a library director or board could easily determine whether a branch is underperforming, achieving expectations, or exceeding expectations.

Organization of the Book

The American public library is a little more than 100 years old, but until the last twenty years, there has been little discussion among library professionals about the need to demonstrate the value of the public library. And while there has been considerable discussion of this topic recently, there still is no unifying theory of or approach to the most effective manner to demonstrate value. Thus, for some stakeholders, especially funding decision makers, the library is viewed as a resource drain. But for others the library is an investment that pays large and wonderful dividends that enrich the local community and America as a whole.

This book provides a compendium of valuable information about the research and literature concerning the issue of demonstrating the value of the public library. The intention has been to integrate this wealth of information into a set of tools that can be easily applied by the public librarian.

Chapter 2—The Grail of Library Goodness

The challenge of demonstrating effectiveness is aggravated by the wide range of services offered as well as the transition to the public library providing access to a combination of print and electronic resources (the hybrid library). Historically librarians have chosen to use input, process, and output measures, subjectively selected by the librarian in an attempt to demonstrate the "goodness" of the public library. This internally focused perspective is much less important than being able to establish the effectiveness of the library from the perspective of the user. Ultimately, the challenge of demonstrating effectiveness is based on the need to focus on the difference the public library makes in the lives of individuals and in the community itself.

Chapter 3—Mission, Values, Vision, and Strategy

Although a majority of public libraries create mission statements, probably fewer than half articulate the values that shape the mission statement and articulate a vision of the future. Yet without such a framework it is difficult to answer two fundamental questions: Who are we? Where are we going? Once a public library has identified the response to these two questions, it can choose from a number of potential strategies to move the library along so that it fulfill its vision. Then the library is able to share with library users, staff, and funding decision makers so that all will have a clear understanding of the library's goals and objectives. And unless the library embraces a planning process that incorporates the library's mission statement and vision statement, has a customer orientation, and identifies the strategies needed to move toward the vision, the public library will likely continue to provide the "same old" services.

Chapter 4—Public Library Users

Having a clear understanding of the demographics of the population surrounding the public library as well as an understanding of the characteristics of users of the library will assist the library in planning for and responding to the needs of users. Other factors, such as the location of the library, also influence the use of a particular library facility.

Chapter 5—Input, Process, and Output Measures

The selection of performance measures is vital so that public library managers will have a clearer picture of the effects of their services on their customers, and funding decision makers will have more confidence that the citizens of a community are being well served. Well-chosen input, process, and output measures, as well as satisfaction and service quality measures, can present an essential perspective on just how well the public library is doing. Tracking the same measures over time allows the library and its stakeholders to know if use of its services is declining or increasing. In short, it is important to demonstrate economy or efficiency in operation as well as providing "value" to the community.

Chapter 6—Outcomes or Benefits of a Public Library

This chapter demonstrates that there is an array of methods to attempt to determine the value of a library and the services that it provides. It is clear that a public library is going to have difficulty assessing its value to individual users, businesses, and the community itself. However, there are methods available to assist the library in identifying its possible social and economic benefits.

Chapter 7—Social Benefits

The attractiveness of social benefits for public libraries is that they have a strong emotional appeal both for library professionals as well as for library stakeholders. However, it is challenging to find measures that go beyond the counting of activities. In short, it is problematic to find a link between specific library services and positive outcomes for an individual or the community. And without this link the assertion of social benefits that arise from the use of the public library is just that: claims.

Chapter 8—Economic Impacts

It is very demanding to ascertain what economic benefits occur from public library use in the lives of customers and the cumulative financial impact on the local community. Although a number of approaches have been suggested and used, none clearly captures all the economic benefits of the public library. Approaches to ascertaining the total economic benefits of a public library are identified and discussed in this chapter. In addition, methods to distinguish the impacts of specific services on the individual and the community are also presented.

Chapter 9—Putting It All Together

Depending on the circumstances and needs of the local community, the public library will plan for and deliver a specific set of services. These may include access to a collection of books and audiovisual materials that will appeal to the leisure time pursuits of the local citizens, services to young children and students, and reference.

To better understand how well the services of the public library are meeting the needs of its users and not meeting the needs of nonusers, it is suggested that the library needs to develop a "culture of assessment." This assessment culture can more effectively choose and analyze a specific set of performance measures that will reflect the actual performance of the library. A variety of ways are available to present these measures, including the use of a balanced scorecard, a library scorecard, and a library index, among others.

Chapter 10—Communicating Value

The experiences and expertise of the city council or county board of supervisors, and their use of and knowledge about the public library, will vary, so the library should select a set of performance measures that will reflect the services that the library provides, then format the information contained in the performance indicators in a way that is appealing to the local stakeholders. In short, the challenge for librarians is to effectively communicate the value, impacts, or dividends of the local public library. Practicing presentation skills and using stories that have a real impact can enhance this communication process.

This book does not present specific information about the how to construct surveys, focus groups and other methodologies that can be used to gather data for performance measures because there are a number of excellent resources already available to provide such advice.[13]

Summary

The problem confronting a library director is that simple numeric measures that are relatively quick and easy to calculate will likely give either an incomplete or a misleading picture of the actual performance of the public library. More meticulous approaches are usually too complex and time consuming for library staff to collect on a regular basis.

Thus, the purpose of this book is to review the various approaches that have been used in assessing the value of the public library and to suggest methods a library might use to develop a better means of communicating with its funding decision makers and other stakeholders. As social organizations, public libraries must be evaluated from the perspective of the impact or benefits that library services provide for users and the community. And the results of the evaluation process must be communicated in terms that can be understood by nonlibrarians—in short, the library's stakeholders.

Notes

1. Eric Donaldson. Delegates Create Policy Proposals for Improved Library and Information Services. *Discovery: The Newspaper of the 1991 White House Conference on Libraries and Information Services,* August 1991, 2.

2. Public Library Association. Standards Committee. *Minimum Standards for Public Library Systems, 1966.* Prepared by the Standards Committee and Subcommittees of the Public Library Association, American Library Association. Adopted July 13, 1966, by the members of the Public Library Association. Chicago: American Library Association, 1967.

3. Douglas Zweizig and Eleanore Jo Rodger. *Output Measures for Public Libraries: A Manual of Standardized Procedures.* Chicago: American Library Association, 1982; Nancy Van House, Mary Jo Lynch, Charles McClure, Douglas Zweizig, and Eleanore Jo Rodger. *Output Measures for Public Libraries.* Chicago: American Library Association, 1987; Charles McClure, Amy Owen, Douglas Zweizig, Mary Jo Lynch, and Nancy Van House. *Planning and Role Setting for Public Libraries.* Chicago: American Library Association, 1987; Thomas A. Childers and Nancy A. Van House. *What's Good: Describing Your Public Library's Effectiveness.* Chicago: American Library Association, 1993.

4. Roswitha Poll. Measuring the Impact and Outcome of Libraries. *Performance Measurement and Metrics*, 4 (1), 2003, 5–12.

5. Daniel O. O'Connor. Evaluating Public Libraries Using Standard Scores: The Library Quotient. *Library Research*, 4, 1982, 51–70.

6. For more about the HAPLR ratings, visit http://www.haplr-index.com/HAPLR100.htm.

7. Jim Scheppke. The Trouble with Hennen. *Library Journal*, 124 (19), November 15 1999, 36–37.

8. Keith Curry Lance and Marti A. Cox. Lies, Damn Lies, and Indexes. *American Libraries*, 31 (6), June/July 2000, 82–86.

9. Barry McIntyre. Measuring Excellence in Public Libraries. *Australian Public Libraries & Information Services*, 7 (3), September 1994, 135–55.

10. Larry Nash White. *Does Counting Count: An Evaluative Study of the Use and Impact of Performance Measurement in Florida Public Libraries.* Tallahassee: Florida State University, 2002.

11. Peter Brewer. Putting Strategy into the Balanced Scorecard. *Strategic Finance*, 83 (7), January 2002, 44–52.

12. Jerilyn R. Veldof. Data Driven Decisions: Using Data to Inform Process Changes in Libraries. *Library & Information Science Research*, 21 (1), 1999, 31–46.

13. See, for example, Thomas Childers and Nancy A. Van House. *What's Good? Describing Your Public Library's Effectiveness.* Chicago: American Library Association, 1993; Rowena Cullen. Perspectives on User Satisfaction Surveys. *Library Trends*, 49 (4), Spring 2001, 662–86; DMA Planning and Management Services. *The Library's Contribution to Your Community: A Resource Manual for Libraries to Document Their Social and Economic Contribution to the Local Community.* Toronto: Southern Ontario Library Service, 1998; Leslie Fitch and Jody Warner. Dividends: The Value of Public Libraries in Canada. *The Bottom Line*, 11 (4), 1998, 158–79; Peter Hernon and Ellen Altman. *Assessing Service Quality: Satisfying the Expectations of Library Customers.* Chicago: American Library Association, 1998; Ethel Himmel and William James Wilson. *Planning for Results: A Public Library*

Transformation Process. Chicago: American Library Association, 1998; Keith Curry Lance, Marcia J. Rodney, Nicolle O. Steffen, Suzanne Kaller, Rochelle Logan, Kristine M. Koontz, and Dean K. Jue. *Counting on Results: New Tools for Outcome-Based Evaluation of Public Libraries.* Aurora, CO: Bibliographic Center for Research, 2002; Charles R. McClure, Bruce T. Fraser, Timothy W. Nelson, and Jane B. Robbins. *Economic Benefits and Impacts from Public Libraries in the State of Florida: Final Report to State Library of Florida, Division of Library and Information Services.* Tallahassee: Information Use Management and Policy Institute, Florida State University, January 2001; Nicolle O. Steffan, Keith Curry Lance, and Rochelle Logan. Time to Tell the Whole Story: Outcome-Based Evaluation and the Counting on Results Project. *Public Libraries*, July/August 2002, 222–28; Nicolle O. Steffan and Keith Curry Lance. Who's Doing What: Outcome-Based Evaluation and Demographics in the Counting on Results Project. *Public Libraries*, September/October 2002, 271–79.

Chapter 2

The Grail of Library Goodness

The whole picture of library goodness requires both a paint-by-numbers approach and impression.—Thomas A. Childers and Nancy A. Van House[1]

Public libraries have always been infused with positive, warm rosy feelings on the part of the public. When cities and other government agencies ask residents to rate various services, the public library nearly always comes out on top (or very near the top). For many, the goodness of the public library is ranked right up there with motherhood and apple pie.

Due to the elusive nature of organizational effectiveness (sometimes called "goodness"), L. B. Mohr has called it the "Holy Grail of management research."[2] The pursuit of the Grail of Library Goodness[3] has led to an overabundance of published and unpublished reports and studies, all attempting to demonstrate the goodness of the library. For public libraries, this search for the Holy Grail has led the profession away from published standards toward a planning process that emphasizes the establishment of goals and objectives and the use of output measures to assess the achievement of those goals. More recently, the planning process has emphasized a possible set of 13 services that can be provided by a public library.[4]

One of the principal differences between a service organization such as a public library and a for-profit business, according to Peter Drucker, is that a business receives resources (it must "earn" its revenues) by satisfying the customer, whereas the service organization receives a budget allocation from a funding source.[5] The problem is that there is little direct relationship between how effective a public library is and the satisfaction experienced by the customer or user. Ultimately, it is not unusual for a budget-based institution such as a public library to judge its effectiveness by the amount of next year's budget allocation. Often, "performance" is the ability to maintain or increase the library's budget. Drucker suggests that service organizations like public libraries should:

1. Answer the question, "What is our business and what should it be?"

2. Derive clear objectives and goals from their definition of function and mission.

3. Identify priorities of concentration that enable them to select targets, set deadlines, and make someone accountable for results.

4. Define measurements of performance.

5. Build feedback from results into their systems.

6. Perform an audit of objectives and results to identify those objectives that no longer serve a useful purpose.

Thomas Childers and Nancy Van House[6] make a similar observation about the lack of a connection between services offered and the availability of revenues:

- Revenues and outputs are separated.

- The lack of a common metric (the bottom line in corporations) is lacking in public sector organizations.

- The decision-making process is bigger than the library.

- The library has neither champions nor foes.

- Library benefits are not widely self-evident.

Another problem associated with assessing the goodness of the library is based on two different values. Librarians are primarily concerned about providing access to resources and information using quality public service staff. As such, librarians have an internal focus and see themselves as "doing good"; they are less concerned about assessing outputs and impacts. The library's funding decision makers have an external view and want to ensure that the library is operating efficiently and effectively—that is, meeting the needs of the local community.

We should be a bit wary of the little library right in the middle of the country. For when it is good, it is very, very good and when it is bad, it's a "pretty good library for a town this size."—Eleanor Jo Rodger[7]

The primary challenges that must be confronted when considering organizational effectiveness include the definition, measurement, and determinants of effectiveness. Quite clearly, the definition of effectiveness is going to be multidimensional since a single perspective is not likely to do justice to any organization. The definition of effectiveness also is going to vary not only by type of organization but also by the choices that a public library makes in terms of the services that it decides to offer and strategies employed to provide those services.

Four models of effectiveness have been identified in management literature:

- The *goal model, goal attainment model,* or *rational system model* views effectiveness in terms of achievement of specific goals and objectives. The focus is on productivity and outputs. Establishing goals may be arbitrary or subjective. This perspective is reflected in such publications as *Output Measures for Public Libraries, Planning and Role Setting for Public Libraries,* and *Planning for Results.*

- The *internal process* or *natural systems model* sees an organization seeking to achieve goals as well as desiring to maintain itself as a social unit. Organizational health, stability, internal processes, and the attainment of goals measure effectiveness.

- The *open systems* or *system resource model* focuses on the interdependence of the organization with its environment. The organizational survival and growth is dependent on acquiring resources, in particular budgetary resources, from external groups.

- The *multiple constituencies approach* or *the participant satisfaction model* sees effectiveness as the degree to which the needs of the various constituencies or stakeholders are met. Some of the stakeholders to be satisfied are not going to control needed fiscal resources (which is the system resource model). The challenge with this perspective is to reconcile the often conflicting needs and wishes of different stakeholders.[8]

One of the important implications of these models is that the choice of any one will, of necessity, only capture a portion of the organization described by the model. Other portions of the organization will not be included in the measurement, and thus it will not reflect the performance of the total organization.

> *The financial crisis is looking even worse, but you will be pleased to know that the librarian reports that the library's performance went up a half a point on the library goodness scale last week.*—Michael K. Buckland[9]

Thomas Childers and Nancy Van House conducted a Public Library Effectiveness Study with the goal of identifying the perceptions of seven groups (users, friends, trustees, local officials, community leaders, library managers, and library service staff) of what performance measures indicate the effectiveness of a public library. As noted in Table 2.1, six items were found in the top ten preferences for all of the groups: convenience of hours, range of materials, range of services, staff helpfulness, services suited to community, and materials quality.

Quite obviously there are more similarities than differences when looking at the indicators across all groups. It is interesting, however, to compare and contrast the responses of users to all of the other groups. Users' preferences seem reasonable. A good library is one that is open at convenient times, has a good range of materials and services, and has helpful staff members. Notice particularly that library staff place greater importance on different criteria of goodness than do the other groups.

The other picture that emerges is that each group has a slightly different perspective that must, in part, be recognized as the public library struggles to put together a set of performance measures to demonstrate the value of the library to all stakeholders.

Using the responses from the survey noted above, the statistical technique factor analysis was used by Childers and Van House to identify eight broad dimensions of effectiveness: outputs and inputs, internal processes, community fit, access to materials, physical facilities, management elements, service offerings, and service to special groups. It is then possible to sort these eight dimensions into one of the four organizational effectiveness models previously noted.

Clearly the goal model and the system resource model have the preponderance of the performance measures that have been developed by librarians as a way to demonstrate the value or effectiveness of the public library, as shown in Table 2.2 (page 18). However, librarians and interested stakeholders should recognize that other perspectives exist and should be used in some situations.

Table 2.1. Top 15 Effectiveness Indicators, Ranked by Each Group

Community Leaders	Local Officials	Trustees	Friends	Users	Library Managers	Service Librarians
1. **Convenience of hours**	Convenience of hours	Convenience of hours	Convenience of hours	Convenience of hours	Convenience of hours	Staff helpfulness
2. **Range of materials**	Range of materials	Staff helpfulness	Range of materials	Range of materials	Staff helpfulness	Range of services
3. **Range of services**	Services suited	Services suited	Staff helpfulness	Range of services	Range of materials	Range of materials
4. **Staff helpfulness**	Range of services	Range of materials	Range of services	Staff helpfulness	Services suited	Convenience of hours
5. Services suited	Staff helpfulness	Range of services	Services suited	Materials quality	Range of services	Services suited
6. **Materials quality**	Materials availability	Public opinion	Convenience of location	Convenience of location	Circulation	Circulation
7. **Materials availability**	Convenience of location	Managerial competence	Materials quality	Materials availability	Public opinion	Materials quality
8. **Awareness of services**	Materials quality	Staff morale	Community well-being	Service freeness	Materials quality	Staff morale
9. **Convenience of location**	Awareness of services	Materials quality	Awareness of services	Services suited	Number of visits	Awareness of services
10. Service freeness	Staff quality	Staff quality	Materials Availability	Newness of materials	Awareness of services	Staff quality
11. **Community well-being**	Community well-being	Users' evaluation	Service freeness	Parking	Convenience of location	Public opinion
12. Users' evaluation	Public opinion	Awareness of services	Staff quality	Speed of services	Staff quality	Number of visits
13. Speed of service	Number of visits	Number of visits	Building easy to identify	Interlibrary cooperation	Users' evaluation	Convenience of location
14. **Staff quality**	Managerial competence	Users' evaluation	Public opinion	Handicapped access	Users per capita	Users' evaluation
15. **Public opinion**	Speed of services	Convenience of location	Special group services	Awareness of services	Materials availability	Materials expended

Note: **Boldface** in the body of the table indicates similar (not identical) rankings in four or more groups

Table 2.2. Public Library Performance Measures

Goal Model	Process Model	System Resource Model	Multiple Constituencies
Outputs and inputs	Internal processes	Outputs and inputs	Community fit
Community fit	Management elements	Internal processes	
Access to materials		Physical facilities	
Service offerings		Management elements	
Service to special groups			

The Public Library Effectiveness Study was replicated in New Zealand, and the results of the survey rankings and the factor analysis were similar to those identified in the United States.[10] People in most of the groups surveyed recognized that perceptions of effectiveness are multidimensional and that a number of measures will be needed when communicating the value of the public library to stakeholders. And although there are no differences in the perceptions of public library effectiveness between geographical areas, no one model of organizational effectiveness dominates among the perceptions of various stakeholders.[11] The good news is that librarians, users, and city council members have relatively congruent views about what constitutes an effective public library. However, it should be recognized that since the public library is a social creation, librarians should involve multiple stakeholders in a process to identify possible measures of a library's "goodness."

Evaluation is the assessment of goodness. It consists of comparing the organization's current performance against some standard or set of expectations. Evaluation has two parts: the collection of information . . . about the organization's performance; and the comparison of this information to [a] set of criteria. The collection of information is not itself evaluation: a critical component of evaluation is the exercise of judgment in which criteria are applied to the organization's current reality.—Thomas A. Childers and Nancy A. Van House[12]

One of the real problems associated with the woof and warp of performance measurement is that it is interwoven with a series of dichotomies:

- Performance measures and indicators, by definition, measure quantitatively; although public library outcomes are intangible, qualitative, personal, and subjective.

- The performance measures of libraries are not wholly comparable, since public libraries may not be attempting to provide identical services.

- Performance measures have difficulty reflecting the fact that library use is largely self-service.

- Performance measures simplify the complexity and diversity of public library services.

- Performance measures are proxies of the service but become the focus in themselves in some cases.

- Performance measures can be used to control the expectations that others have of the library.

- Some librarians may not want to share performance measures since they may reveal too much about the library and its services.

In short, library stakeholders, in particular funding decision makers, are concerned about understanding the performance of the library from several different perspectives:

- What *goals and objectives* the library is striving to reach and what proportion of the population the library is serving.

- A set of measures that indicate what *progress* is being made to achieve the library's goals and objectives. In most cases, this will be a combination of output and outcome measures.

- *Efficiency measures* that demonstrate that the library is operating efficiently and is a good custodian of the public funds provided by the taxpayers in the community.

- *Trends and comparisons* that show how the library has done over time compared with other comparable libraries.

In a 1996 survey conducted in 500 communities, library directors and public officials differed significantly in their perceptions of the public library and its value to the community when compared to other tax-supported services. Among the public officials, the public library provided a lower "return for tax dollars spent," even when the local library was judged to be close to an ideal public library.[13]

> *A major aspect of library effectiveness is representing the library to key stakeholders.*—Thomas A. Childers and Nancy A. Van House[14]

The use of performance measures in public libraries is most effective when they adhere to the following set of guiding principles:

- *Clarity of purpose.* Since the multiplicity of stakeholders may have different interests and reasons to use the information contained within a set of performance measures, the library should clearly identify their needs.

- *Focus.* The performance measures should indicate not only their current value but also the targets identified by the library so that the various stakeholders will know what progress is being made to achieve the goals and objectives of the library. An important consideration is to make sure that the library's objectives are clearly stated and can, in some manner, be measured.

- *Alignment.* The performance measures that are selected by the library should reflect the service objectives being performed by the library. All library managers and full-time staff members should understand the reasons for the use of the performance measures and how they are being used to communicate the value of the public library.

- *Balance.* The choice of performance measures should reveal how the library transforms the resources that it receives to provide services reflected in the output and outcomes indicators. Most important, the measures should assess the impact of library services on the individual and the community being served. The performance measures should be discussed regularly at staff meetings so that staff members will understand how their actions influence the indicators.

- *Regular refinement.* Although it is important to use indicators and track the performance of the library over time, it is also essential to periodically assess the value of a particular measure because the vision or strategies being used by the library may have changed.

- *Robust performance measures.* Performance measure, although only an approximation of reality, should accurately measure what is intended. The set of measures should make sense and be easily understood, especially by the various library stakeholders. Measures should be clearly defined to ensure consistent collection, as well as being unambiguous.[15]

Clearly no single measure of library goodness is going to fulfill the expectations of the multiple groups that need to be satisfied. Without a clear understanding of and agreement on the mission and vision of the library, there may be conflicts over how well the goals of the library are actually achieved. The reality is that the public library is controlled to a large extent by the resources available to it (and the public library does not have direct control over the allocation of these resources). Providing the tools and resources allows a well-trained staff to provide services in an efficient manner.

In the past, little was required of a public library beyond having the library director adhere to its budget allocations. In such an environment there was little encouragement and few rewards for being "good" beyond personal satisfaction. While public library stakeholders, including the funding decision makers, have historically accepted the conventional wisdom of the "community goodness" provided by the library, stakeholders are increasingly demanding tangible proof that the public library is delivering quality library services that meet the needs of the community using cost-efficient means. The bottom line is a demand for increased accountability.

This demand is not new. Back in 1973, R. H. Orr suggested that libraries needed to focus on providing answers to three "goodness" questions:

- How good is the library?

- How good is the library management?

- What good does the library do?[16]

Yet public librarians have difficulty deciding how to approach this issue of reporting performance, for several reasons:

- *Lack of consensus.* The library profession has not spoken with one "clear voice" about what performance measures should be used to report the library's accomplishments.

- *Lack of definitions.* The library profession has failed to adopt a consistent set of definitions for the plethora of performance measures that already exist. The result is that two libraries can be reporting the same statistic and actually be measuring two different perspectives on a service, be collecting the data differently, and so forth.

- *Lack of understanding.* Public library directors and managers often have a poor understanding of the potential value and utility of performance measures that when consistently applied can assist in improving the operation of the library. As such, these individuals are ambivalent toward evaluation in general and specifically toward the difficulty of attempting to assess the outputs of the public library on the individual user and the local community.

- *Lack of structure.* There may be several reasons that prevent public libraries from effectively using performance measures. Among these are the library's culture, a desire not to waste time and resources, the need for staff to become more knowledgeable, and the need for training.

- *Statistical overload.* Most public libraries collect a great many performance measures. The state library and federal surveys often mandate the collection of some statistics, while the local library continues to gather other measures it has "always" collected. As such, staff members are more than likely to be overwhelmed by the prospect of collecting some "new" performance measures without considering the possibility of deciding to stop collecting others.

As a result, the library profession has been unable to answer even such basic questions as:

- What is a good public library?

- What is a bad public library?

- How can you move from being "bad" to being "good?"

Summary

Demonstrating the "goodness" of the public library, which historically librarians have focused on through their use of input, process, and output measures, is much less important than being able to establish the effectiveness of the library from the perspective of the user. This challenge of demonstrating effectiveness is being exacerbated by the wide range of services offered by public libraries as well as the transition from the traditional print-based library to the public library providing access to a combination of print and electronic resources (the hybrid library).

In addition, the public library must overcome the inertia of continuing to do what it has always done while resisting calls to provide relevant information about the utility of the public library. Historically, and today, the generally accepted folk wisdom has usually regarded the public library as a good thing. Yet folk wisdom is no substitute for demonstrating the relevance of the library to its stakeholders, especially the mayors, city managers, county administrators, and boards who control the library's purse strings. Ultimately, the challenge of demonstrating effectiveness is based on the need to focus on the difference the public library makes in the lives of individuals and in the community itself.

Notes

1. Thomas Childers and Nancy A. Van House. *What's Good? Describing Your Public Library's Effectiveness.* Chicago: American Library Association, 1993.

2. L. B. Mohr. *Explaining Organizational Behavior: The Limits and Possibilities of Theory and Research.* San Francisco: Jossey-Bass, 1982.

3. Michael Buckland. *Library Services in Theory and Context.* New York: Pergamon, 1988, 241.

4. Ethel Himmel and William James Wilson. *Planning for Results: A Public Library Transformation Process.* Chicago: American Library Association, 1998.

5. Peter F. Drucker. Managing the Public Service Institution. *The Public Interest*, 33, Fall 1973, 43–60.

6. Childers and Van House. *What's Good?*

7. Eleanor Jo Roger. Performance Measurement and Public and Public Library Goodness. *New Zealand Libraries*, 46 (4), March 1990, 17–20.

8. Thomas Childers and Nancy Van House. The Grail of Goodness: The Effective Public Library. *Library Journal*, 114, October 1, 1989, 44–49; Thomas Childers and Nancy Van House. Dimensions of Public Library Effectiveness. *Library and Information Science Review*, 11, 1989, 273–301; Nancy Van House and Thomas Childers. Dimensions of Public Library Effectiveness II: Library Performance. *Library and Information Science Review*, 12, 1990, 131–53.

9. Michael K. Buckland. Concepts of Library Goodness. *Canadian Library Journal*, 39 (2), April 1982, 63–66.

10. Rowena J. Cullen and Philip J. Calvert. Further Dimensions of Public Library Effectiveness: Report of a Parallel New Zealand Study. *Library and Information Science Review*, 15, 1993, 143–64; Philip J. Calvert and Rowena J. Cullen. Further Dimensions of Public Library Effectiveness II: The Second Stage of the New Zealand Study. *Library and Information Science Review*, 16, 1994, 87–104.

11. Philip J. Calvert and Rowena J. Cullen. Performance Measurement in New Zealand Public Libraries: A Research Project. *Australasian Public Library & Information Services*, 5 (1), March 1992, 3–12; Philip J. Calvert and Rowena J. Cullen. The New Zealand Public Libraries Effectiveness Study and the New Zealand University Libraries Effectiveness Study. *Australian Academic & Research Libraries*, 26 (2), June 1995, 97–106.

12. Childers and Van House. *What's Good?*, 9

13. Leigh Estabrook and Edward Lakner. A Survey of Public Libraries and Local Government. *Illinois State Library: Special Report Series*, 4, 1997, 5–62.

14. Childers and Van House. *What's Good?*

15. The Audit Commission. *Aiming to Improve: The Principles of Performance Measurement*. London: The Audit Commission, 2000.

16. R. H. Orr. Measuring the Goodness of Library Services: A General Framework for Considering Quantitative Measures. *Journal of Documentation*, 29 (3), September 1973, 315–32.

Chapter

3

Mission, Values, Vision, and Strategy

The public library of the 1990s is driven by two goals: providing recreational reading material and providing information. The strain of trying to excel in both areas results in neither goal being completely fulfilled.—Leah K. Starr[1]

Historically, many organizations including public libraries have used a planning process to develop long-range plans, goals, and objectives. One of the more popular approaches is to use the mission statement of the library as a starting point. Using a top-down approach allows the library to link the library's mission and vision to the strategies that it will use to achieve the vision (see Figure 3.1). Given the premise that "what gets measured gets done," an inadequate performance measurement system can have adverse consequences for any public library.

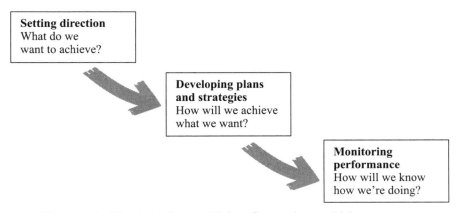

Setting direction
What do we
want to achieve?

**Developing plans
and strategies**
How will we achieve
what we want?

**Monitoring
performance**
How will we know
how we're doing?

Figure 3.1. Aligning Mission, Vision, Strategies, and Measurement

25

Mission Statement

The typical mission statement is a long, awkward sentence [paragraph, or page] that demonstrates management's inability to think clearly.—Scott Adams[2]

Each public library should periodically review and update its mission statement to ensure that it reflects the needs of its community. Surprisingly, a visit to Hennen's American Public Library Ratings Web site found that less than half of these exemplar public libraries had a mission statement that could be found on each library's Web site. A review of the available mission statements found that among the more popular phrases in these statements were "positive difference," "providing materials, information, and services," "equal access," and "welcoming environments," as shown in Table 3.1 (page 28). A sample of public library mission statement's is provided in Figure 3.2. Surprisingly, after a mention of customer, citizen, patron, and community, only half of the mission statements mentioned "materials, information and services" to meet an "educational, recreational and informational need." Perhaps the most charitable summation of these mission statements is that they are simply too long and not very memorable.

The process of long-range planning—in some organizations it might be called strategic planning, program planning, business planning, or direction planning—clarifies why the public library exists, who it exists for, what services and products are provided to different groups of clients, how these products and services will be evaluated, and where it is going.[3] This generalized view of the planning process is illustrated in Figure 3.3 (page 29) and demonstrates the interdependent relationships among each of the components.

The mission of the Salt Lake County Library System is to make a positive difference in the lives of our customers by responsively providing materials, information, and services at community libraries located throughout the Salt Lake Valley and/or via the Library's World Wide Web site.

The mission of the San Diego Public Library is to:

Respond to the information needs of San Diego's diverse communities.

Ensure equal access to local, national, and global resources.

Anticipate and address the educational, cultural, business, and recreational interests of the public.

Develop and provide welcoming environments.

Multnomah County Library serves the people of Multnomah County by providing books and other materials to meet their informational, educational, cultural and recreational needs.

The Multnomah County Library upholds the principles of intellectual freedom and the public's right to know by providing people of all ages with access and guidance to information and collections that reflect all points of view.

The Cuyahoga County Public Library will provide our communities free and open access to information giving every person the opportunity for enrichment, inspiration, and entertainment.

To provide and to encourage the use of library resources and services where the Fairfax County Public Library can best meet the evolving educational, recreational, and informational needs of all the residents of Fairfax County and Fairfax City, thus enhancing individual and community life.

The Santa Clara County Library is an open forum promoting knowledge, ideas, and cultural enrichment. The library provides free access to informational, educational, and recreational materials and services. In response to community needs, the library provides diverse resources on a wide variety of subjects and viewpoints and helps people use these resources.

The mission of the Richland County Free Library (SC) is meeting our citizens' needs for reading, learning and information.

The Toledo-Lucas County Public Library supports and enhances a better quality of life for all residents of Lucas County. This is achieved by offering open and equitable access to information and services in a variety of formats and locations.

Figure 3.2. Sample Public Library Mission Statements *(Continued)*

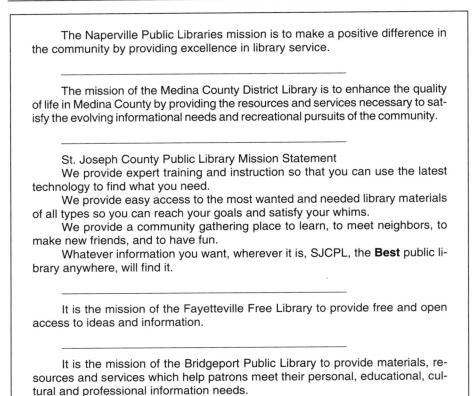

The Naperville Public Libraries mission is to make a positive difference in the community by providing excellence in library service.

The mission of the Medina County District Library is to enhance the quality of life in Medina County by providing the resources and services necessary to satisfy the evolving informational needs and recreational pursuits of the community.

St. Joseph County Public Library Mission Statement
We provide expert training and instruction so that you can use the latest technology to find what you need.
We provide easy access to the most wanted and needed library materials of all types so you can reach your goals and satisfy your whims.
We provide a community gathering place to learn, to meet neighbors, to make new friends, and to have fun.
Whatever information you want, wherever it is, SJCPL, the **Best** public library anywhere, will find it.

It is the mission of the Fayetteville Free Library to provide free and open access to ideas and information.

It is the mission of the Bridgeport Public Library to provide materials, resources and services which help patrons meet their personal, educational, cultural and professional information needs.

Figure 3.2. Sample Public Library Mission Statements

Table 3.1. Five Recurring Phrases in Mission Statements

Phrase	Occurrence
Customers/citizens/people/patrons/residents/community	66%
Providing materials, information, and services	53%
Educational, recreational, and informational needs	47%
Free and open access	40%
Enhancing individual and community life	33%

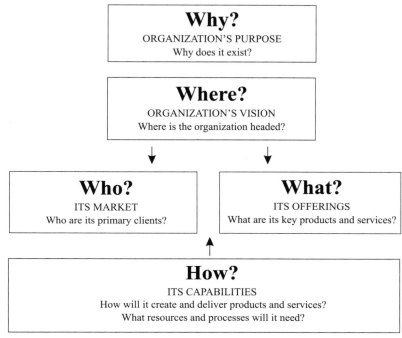

Figure 3.3. Planning Framework

A good planning process will ensure that the following five components have been carefully addressed:

- **Rationale**. Why does the public library exist? Why does the library continue to provide services? What is the organization's mission statement?
- **Vision**. Where is the public library headed? What is the appropriate role for the library to play in its community?
- **Market**. What groups does the library serve? Do remote users have access to the same set of resources as those who physically visit the public library?
- **Offerings**. What products and services does the public library provide?
- **Capabilities**. What resources—technology, space, people, and processes—are required to provide the services and products the library offers?

The clarity of the library's mission statement is crucial so that all staff members have a clear understanding of the goals and direction of the organization. A mission statement should

- define what the library does and does not do,
- distinguish the organization from the competition,

- be no more than a short paragraph in length (one sentence is better),
- be written in plain English and employ no buzzwords,
- lead to clear actions, and
- focus on the present (it's not a future-focused vision statement).

The purpose of the mission statement is to clearly articulate the public library's role in its community. Attempts to craft a public library's mission statement by committee will likely result in something less than inspiring. A review of the public library mission statements included in Figure 3.2 suggests that many are simply too long, often employ library jargon, and are not very memorable.

Vision and Values Statement

> *Vision comes from the heart, not the head. Our purpose in creating the vision is to clarify what we wish to create, knowing all along that we may never get there.*—Peter Block[4]

The vision statement sets out long-term targets and success criteria for the library and acts as a focus for identifying the key strategic activities that must be accomplished if the vision is to be achieved.[5] A good vision statement is clear, memorable, motivating, and customer-related and can be translated into measurable strategies. If a vision statement is too long, it will fail the test of being memorable. And unless the vision is focused on meeting customer needs, the reason for the library is being ignored.

> *Without vision the people perish.*—Prov. 29:18

As a part of the process to identify and create a vision, the public library should consider that it could be viewed from a number of perspectives. Among the more noteworthy perspectives are the following:

- *A physical collection.* The library is a collection of materials with a variety of formats: books, journals, audiovisual, microforms, documents, maps, and so forth.
- *Nurturer of the independent learner.* The library provides support for the independent learner, particularly adults interested in broadening their horizons.

- *Knowledge navigator.* In addition to providing traditional in-library reference service, the library can also provide a form of online 24/7 reference. This can be complemented by providing and updating a variety of pathfinders.

- *Information technology provider.* The library provides access to information and computer technology as well as staff with superior information management skills.

- *Document deliverer.* The library delivers documents, in particular copies of journal articles, using interlibrary loan and links to document delivery firms.

- *Meeting place.* The public library provides access to meeting rooms of varying sizes to facilitate a broader sense of community.

- *Educator of students.* The public library assists in developing information management or information literacy skills as well as providing resources that help students complete assignments.

- *Filterer, evaluator, and selector of information resources* (physical and electronic). The library becomes a "preferred" information intermediary known for providing access to quality information resources. As the library moves toward providing more electronic resources it becomes more of an "invisible" intermediary, sometimes called a portal.

- *Information provider.* The library provides access to its collection and skilled professional librarians to assist users in meeting their information needs. In some cases, the library focuses on collecting and organizing information about social and other services that are available within the community.

- *Memory institution.* Although the role of preserving materials is often associated with museums and large academic libraries, public libraries will, in some cases, be active in this role, especially for local historical materials.

A large survey of U.S. patrons in several communities noted that these individuals believed the local library served three primary roles in the community: educational support, provision of information, and providing access to recreational materials.[6]

The Cerritos (California) Public Library decided to change the focus of its library services and based its planning on understanding how the user would *experience* service. This meant that the library collections, technology, policies, staffing, and training were all reworked from the experience perspective.[7] The library district in London's East End decided to close seven branch libraries and replace them with seven radically new "Idea Stores" to eliminate the perception of the library as a quaint, outdated, and obsolete institution. These libraries are using retail-style branding and image promotion to more aggressively market themselves.[8]

Leadership is the capacity to translate vision into reality. Top library managers must clearly convey the organization's mission, strategic direction, and vision to employees, customers, and funding decision makers. A clear, concise statement that communicates what the organization is and is not increases the likelihood of buy-in from both employees and stakeholders.

As noted previously, only about half of the libraries found on Hennen's Web site have included a mission statement that can be found in the public library's Web site. Even fewer libraries have included a vision statement on their Web sites. A sample of public library vision statements may be found in Figure 3.4. Unfortunately, it is difficult to distinguish between the vision and mission statements in these public library examples.

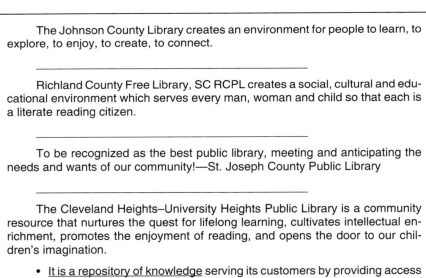

    The Johnson County Library creates an environment for people to learn, to explore, to enjoy, to create, to connect.

    Richland County Free Library, SC RCPL creates a social, cultural and educational environment which serves every man, woman and child so that each is a literate reading citizen.

    To be recognized as the best public library, meeting and anticipating the needs and wants of our community!—St. Joseph County Public Library

---

    The Cleveland Heights–University Heights Public Library is a community resource that nurtures the quest for lifelong learning, cultivates intellectual enrichment, promotes the enjoyment of reading, and opens the door to our children's imagination.

- It is a repository of knowledge serving its customers by providing access to information from any available source, including physical and electronic material;

- It is a center for literacy development and intellectual growth that teaches and encourages its customers to access, evaluate and use print, electronic and other information sources so they can transform information into usable knowledge;

- It is a community-gathering place for public forums and group meetings, educational courses, programs for children and adults, senior citizen activities and recreational reading and learning. It is the focal point for information technologies for its communities. It actively promotes the cities its serves;

Figure 3.4. Sample Public Library Vision Statements   *(Continued)*

- It is the leading library system of its size in the nation, a customer service-oriented pace-setter through its:

  Breadth, depth and accessibility of services for its customers;

  Approaches to library services using innovative technology and techniques;

  Services to customer groups with special needs and interests;

  Establishment and enforcement of evaluative processes to measure quality of services.

- This vision will be attained through the commitment of a well-trained, diverse, empowered staff determined to make it happen. We share responsibility and decision-making through teamwork and cooperation.

The Cleveland Heights–University Heights Public Library is a bridge into the future. Generous community support and funding translates this vision into reality.

The Bettendorf Public Library Information Center will be the recognized source of knowledge and information, the place to gather and discuss, the encourager of reading, and the leader in cooperation with the city, schools and organizations. We will be the gateway to life-long learning, offering a full spectrum of services, materials and programming.

The Darien Library Vision—Our vision is to inform, educate, entertain, and enrich our community.

Figure 3.4. Sample Public Library Vision Statements

It is interesting to compare and contrast these library vision statements with those from private industry and nonprofit organizations, as shown in Table 3.2. Note that being "Favorite, best, top, or first choice" is the most frequently occurring phrase among companies and nonprofit organizations, yet the author was only able to find one public library—St. Joseph County Public Library—whose vision includes being the "best." Interesting!

Table 3.2. Recurring Phrases in Vision Statements

	Companies	Nonprofits
Favorite/best/top/first choice	38%	19%
Customer/client/consumer	31%	25%
Lead/leader	24%	6%
Selective	12%	
Most successful	10%	

Adapted from Hugh Davidson. *The Committed Enterprise: How to Make Vision and Values Work.* New York: Butterworth Heinemann, 2002, 89.

Since the values of an organization support the vision, a clear articulation of these values is helpful for staff and the library's customers. Examples of the values likely to found within a public library are noted in Figure 3.5.

Public Library Values

The Cuyahoga County Public Library is committed to . . .
1) Providing free, open, and equitable service to all persons.
2) Providing the best possible access to a wide variety of materials.
3) Respecting each and every customer.
4) Respecting each other as the organization's most important resource.
5) Valuing and supporting diversity of people and perspectives.
6) Being skilled and dedicated to customer service.
7) Focusing on continuous learning and innovation.
8) Being responsible stewards of public funds.
9) Being accountable for our performance.
10) Keeping our promises to our communities and ourselves.

Salt Lake County Library Value Statement.
Service to customers is our highest priority. Consequently, we value:

PEOPLE:
We value each customer and staff member and believe each should be given respect and equal treatment.
We value differing points of view as well as cultural and ethnic diversity.
We value opportunity for growth and recognition.

INTEGRITY:
We value fairness, honesty, trust, accountability and ethical conduct.
We value the demonstration of individual responsibility for actions by library customers and staff.

EXCELLENCE:
We value competence, professionalism and the empowerment of our staff.
We value the provision of staff training and continuing education.
We value staff striving towards continuous improvement and the provision of exceptional customer service.

EQUALITY OF SERVICE:
We value responsiveness to the needs of all customers, and convenient access to a variety of materials and services using the resources of the entire library system.

Figure 3.5. Sample Public Library Values   *(Continued)*

CREATIVITY:
> We value personal initiative, problem solving, enthusiasm, responsible risk taking, planning for future needs, and the effective use of technology and other library resources.

EFFICIENCY:
> We value efficient use of taxpayer's dollars and seek to reduce operating costs whenever possible through more efficient methods.

LIBRARY ENVIRONMENT:
> We value safe, clean, comfortable, functional, accessible and aesthetically pleasing buildings and surroundings.

In some cases, a library's values are expressed as a:

Patron Bill of Rights

- The staff of the Naperville Public Libraries strives to provide patrons with a highly satisfying library experience. This involves using excellent customer service to maintain a long-standing partnership between patrons and the Naperville Public Libraries.
- Library patrons receive prompt, friendly, courteous, and respectful service at all times.
- Library patrons are entitled to have the privacy of their library records and information safeguarded by Library Staff.
- Library patrons are able to check out books and other materials, register for library cards, and pay fines & fees without undue delays.
- Library patrons are entitled to equitable service regardless of age, gender, ethnicity, religion, race, appearance or disability.
- Library patrons are entitled to an empowered staff to make the library system work for them.
- Library patrons' telephone calls are not transferred needlessly or left on hold.
- Library patrons are entitled to submit comments and suggestions about all materials and services. They are entitled to timely responses.
- Library patrons are entitled to obtain accurate, timely, useful and current information.
- Library patrons are entitled to education about library procedures and services.
- Library patrons are entitled to individual, professional attention by trained, knowledgeable staff.
- Library patrons are entitled to a clean, comfortable, safe, and well-maintained library environment.
- Library patrons are entitled to an easy-to-use facility including orderly shelves, prompt re-shelving of materials, good lighting, proper signage, and equipment in good working order.

Figure 3.5. Sample Public Library Values

Having a clearly articulated and written vision and set of values provides a perspective on being aware of where you are (and have come from) and knowing where you are heading. Since there are many possible destinations, knowing the desired destination allows the library and its staff members to make better decisions and choices as the future enfolds. Having a specific destination allows the library to focus rather than attempting to be all things to all people (and doing most of these things poorly).

Assessing the environment within which the public library exists is an important first step in any planning process. Assessing the context of the current and likely future environment helps to determine what factors will affect the public library. What trends, government regulations, and technology changes will affect the organization? Who are the library's competitors and how well is your library doing in the competitive environment? One of the most popular planning tools to assist in this process is called SWOT—identifying the strengths, weaknesses, opportunities, and threats to your library, as shown in Table 3.3. An alternative acronym, WOTS UP (weaknesses, opportunities, threats and strengths underlying planning), is sometimes used.

Table 3.3. SWOT Analysis

	Internal (within the library)	External (outside the library)
Positive	Strengths	Opportunities
Negative	Weaknesses	Threats

Typically the SWOT analysis starts with an internal focus. One of the challenges of such an analysis is to try to achieve a balanced and objective perspective. At times it is difficult to identify the strengths and limitations of the library. The quality of the library's collection, staff, infrastructure, services, programs, and funding, for example, may either be a strength or weakness.

Once the internal assessment has been completed, attention shifts to the external focus. Here too it may be difficult to objectively assess what is happening in the external environment without checking a variety of information resources. One helpful technique is to remember to use the mnemonic "temples" when considering the external arena.[9] "Temples" stands for

- *Technology*. What are the important technologies and technology-based standards that might have an impact on the library and its ability to provide new or enhanced services?

- *Economy*. What is happening with the economy, and would a downturn or expansion in the state or local economy have an impact on the library's budget?

- *Markets*. Would the ever-changing marketplace (for information resources and services provided by a public library) create a new competitor or provide a new opportunity for the library? Are Internet-based reference services (ask-a-question) a competitor and/or a threat?

- *Politics*. Is there a change in the political environment that might have an impact on local government? Will a new city council member want to make a change in the library board?

- *Law*. Are there any federal, state, or local laws that might have an impact on the local public library? Changes in administrative law and regulations might also require a change in service offerings at your public library.

- *Ethics*. Are there clear policies regarding how materials and services are acquired by the public library?

- *Society*. Is society changing in ways that require a reexamination of the mission, goals, and vision of the public library? Are the population demographics changing?

Once the issues for each of these areas has been identified and assessed, then the library can determine whether it needs to create or modify a vision statement. Quite clearly the goal for any public library is to remain in "synch" with its community so that it can better serve its citizens. Often sharing a draft of the vision statement with the library's stakeholders will elicit comments and remarks that will allow the library to quickly determine if its vision is "in tune" or "resonates" with the community.

Model Mission and Value Statements

Using the above information about the value and utility of mission and vision statements, it is possible to construct model statements for the typical public library that overcome some of the defects noted above. For example:

> Our mission is to provide access to information resources and library services to our citizens that enhances their quality of life and provides opportunities for personal, community and economic development.

> Our vision is to inform, educate, entertain and enrich our community.

Strategic Aims

> *Think of strategy as a bridge: values are the bedrock on which the piers of the bridge are planted, the near bank is today's reality, the far bank is the vision. Your strategy is the bridge itself.*—Gordon R. Sullivan[10]

Attempts by some organizations to find the "right or correct" strategy—in the hope that that is what is needed to succeed—are not likely to succeed. An examination of why some companies, and their CEOs, have failed leads to the conclusion that the real problem isn't bad strategy but rather bad execution.[11] Michael Porter, a Harvard Business School professor and well-known expert in the area of strategic planning, has noted that strategy cannot be limited to those at the top of an organization but rather must involve all staff members as they go about completing their tasks.[12]

The management literature is replete with definitions of strategy. In general these definitions fall into four categories:

- A *plan* or a means for getting from here to there.

- A *pattern* of actions over time, for example, focusing on a particular market segment.

- A *position* that reflects decisions to offer products and services in particular markets.

- A *perspective*, vision, or direction of what the organization is to become.

A strategy is a plan of action with a shared understanding designed to accomplish a specific goal that focuses on how a given objective will be achieved. Strategies are designed to move the library toward its vision and to eliminate the gap that exists between where the library is today and where it wants to be tomorrow. Strategies are *not* the programmatic goals and objectives that most public libraries have historically developed on an annual basis. For example, some libraries develop programmatic goals that can be grouped into several categories (services, technology, resources, staff development). Such an approach does not reflect a coherent set of strategies but is rather a potpourri of goals and objectives and represents a strategy known as "more of the same."

Strategies are about making choices and deliberately choosing to be different. A strategy allows an organization to create a sustainable advantage. Strategy recognizes that it is not possible to be all things to all people and thus focuses on choices. A more formal definition states that:

Strategy is the direction and scope of an organization over the long term; which achieves advantage for the organization through its configuration of resources within a changing environment, to meet the needs of markets and to fulfill stakeholder expectations.[13]

Ultimately, a strategy is judged by how well it delivers long-term added value for the customers of the organization. How a public library adds value reflects its core competencies and how well it delivers its services to meet the needs of its customers. Identifying the ways in which the public library adds value and what the appropriate strategies for a library to pursue are is the responsibility of the management team of the library. In short, focusing on the "big picture" is much more important than the operational day-to-day crises that seem to occupy so much time of library staff members.

There are three broad strategies that can be considered should a public library wish to be more responsive to its community: operational excellence, customer intimacy, and innovative services.[14] These broad avenues are interconnected, as shown in Figure 3.6. Becoming a master of one of these value disciplines means that the organization can differentiate itself from its competitors.

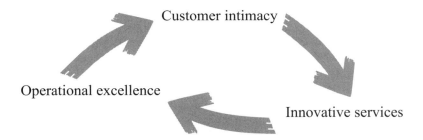

Figure 3.6. Relationships of Broad Strategies

Operational excellence means providing customers with reliable products or services delivered with minimal difficulty or inconvenience. The customer of the public library must make a conscious decision to visit the library (in-person or electronically), whereas other public services, for example, police and fire services, are delivered where and when needed. Examples of companies that have focused on operational excellence are Dell Computers, Wal-Mart, and Federal Express. These organizations are always seeking ways to minimize overhead costs, reduce transaction costs (inconveniences), and reduce departmental boundaries.

When considering operational excellence, some of the questions that should be addressed are:

- What economies of scale exist?
- What level of quality can be attained (quality will likely vary by each library service)?
- How can technology increase efficiencies?
- What changes in procedures and processes will lead to improved productivity?

Customer intimacy means segmenting and targeting markets with tailored offerings to match the needs of that particular niche. An organization will use information about customers, freely provided by the customers, to tailor their service offerings. Some customer intimacy approaches that work effectively are frequent buyer membership clubs, providing optional personalization services such as that found on Amazon.com, and providing different services and different levels of service to various segments of the marketplace.

Focusing on customer intimacy means that several questions should be addressed:

- What is the library's competitive advantage?
- Who is the competition?
- How can we better serve our existing customers?
- What new segments of the population can be targeted?
- What share of the market can we expect given our resources?
- Do we really know what different types of customers want?

Having a greater understanding of the needs of the library's customers and how the library adds value will allow the library to potentially develop *innovative services.* As these services are incorporated into the routine library service offerings, they will be more highly appreciated and valued by the customers of the library. Organizations that focus on product or service leadership do so by recognizing and embracing ideas from outside the organization and then quickly transforming the idea into a service offering.

When considering service innovation, a library should ask:

- If there were no constraints, what could we do?
- How can we take our existing service to a new level?
- What service can we discontinue to reallocate resources?
- What has never been tried before?

- What are the options, new alternatives, and potential synergies that should be considered?

- Would upgrading our technology base provide the library with the potential for introducing new services or improving existing services?

- Does the library have the talent and skills among existing staff to meet the challenge of innovation?

For most libraries, the reality is that there is a total disconnect between the daily actions of managers and the activities of staff members and the library's mission statement and vision for the future. Strategy is not about destination but about the route the library chooses to take—*how* to reach the desired destination. Most important, an effective strategy is one that will differentiate the public library from its competitors.

As noted above, the three broad strategies that a library may follow include operational excellence, customer intimacy, and service leadership (innovative services). Specific strategies that an organization, including the public library, can choose to adopt include:

- **Differentiation.** As noted in the following list, there are a number of ways in which the public library can differentiate itself from its competitors:

  - *Quality.* The public library can provide access to information resources that have been vetted as to their accuracy, timeliness, thoroughness, and so forth. The library's customers know that they will save time when searching for information since the available resources will be of high quality.

  - *Name.* The public library is a brand name, and this "brand" carries with it a certain set of both positive and negative stereotypes or expectations about the library itself. Surprisingly, most public libraries do little to enhance the positive aspects of the public library "brand."

  - *Customer orientation.* The use of the word "customer" in lieu of patron or user suggests that individuals have a choice and can "vote" both with their feet (not returning to the library) and their pocketbooks (not voting in favor of a library tax override or bond issue) should their perception of the service they receive not meet their expectations. The library might embrace a strategy that attempts to provide a more personalized set of services. The library might begin to collect customer preference information as a means of providing these personalized services.

- *Installed customer base.* The public library has a very important asset: information about its customers (name, mailing address, e-mail address, and so forth). This information is rarely used by the library to inform its customers of new services, new materials that might be of interest to the customer, and so forth.

- *Innovation.* Given the plethora of information resources and the competition that public libraries now face, perhaps it is time to consider ways in which the library can innovate and provide clear value to its customers. In private industry, some government agencies, and nonprofit organizations, innovation is the key to the continued success of the organization.

- *Technical superiority.* Perhaps the "key" technical superiority that librarians bring to the table is that they are trained in how to provide access to a diverse body of information resources. The key organizing tool that libraries employ to accomplish this task is to create, maintain, and enhance the library's catalog so that it provides access to high-quality information resources—regardless of their location. Yet the mere fact that libraries have always provided the public catalog means that its contribution is rarely understood or acknowledged. Perhaps this "strength" should be more aggressively marketed by the library to demonstrate one of its value-added activities.

- *Distribution.* Public libraries located in larger communities typically build and maintain branch libraries so that their customers are better served. Information resources are routinely moved from location to location to meet requests from the library's customers. Some libraries are extending their distribution by providing access to the library's collection and 24/7 reference services using the Internet.

- **Changing service offerings in existing markets.** A change in a service offering can be effected in several ways. Among these are

    - *Expanding service offerings.* The public library might introduce a new service to a group within the community previously not served.

    - *Narrowing or refocusing service offerings.* The library might stop providing a service that is infrequently used or is expensive to maintain when compared to the costs of providing other services.

    - *Improving quality of service.* The quality of service could be improved by the time it takes to complete a task, the accuracy of the service, the timeliness of the service, the completeness, and so forth.

- **Increasing service/product usage.** The public library could effect an increase in the usage of a service or product by

  - *Increasing the frequency of usage.* The library might be able to increase the frequency of use of its collection or a service by increasing the value the library customer receives.

  - *Increasing the quantity used.* Library customers might wish to borrow more items each time they visit the library if they are somehow informed of available resources they might find of value.

  - *Finding new applications for current users.* Library customers who currently use the library infrequently might be encouraged to use library services more frequently.

- **Focusing.** Rather than attempting to be all things to all people, the public library might focus on providing one or two service offerings at a particular location. Typically an organization can focus using one of three approaches:

  - *Product/service focus.* The Public Library Association has recommended use of a planning process (see Himmel and Wilson, *Planning for Results*)[15] that suggests that there are 13 service responses a library may choose to focus on (see Figure 3.7, page 44). Obviously no library is going to attempt to tackle all 13 service responses. Rather, the library will typically choose two or three service responses as a focus. Depending on the service alternative selected, the library should acknowledge during the planning process that users and library staff have different roles to play, and that different resources, services, programming, and supporting technologies will be needed, as shown in Table 3.4 (page 45).

    Matthew Simon has developed an alternative list of the possible roles that a public library can play within a community, derived from talking to a large number of library users:

    A community and social center

    A play space

    A study hall

    An economic asset for the community

    A lifelong learning center

    A museum

    A cultural center

A window on the world

A place of energy

A marketing research center.[16]

George D'Elia and Eleanor Jo Rodger reported the results of a large national survey conducted by the Gallup Organization to determine the importance of various roles of the public library among the public and community opinion leaders.[17] The results of this survey are shown in Table 3.5.

- *Geographic focus.* Another option is to focus on providing library services to specific areas of the community. Public libraries have long followed this approach as they build and maintain branch libraries.

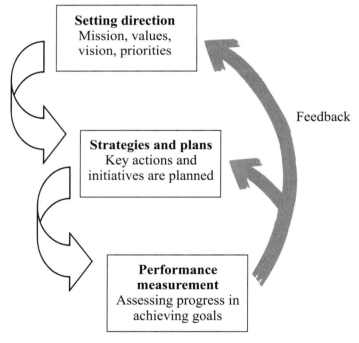

Figure 3.7. Planning Approach

Table 3.4. Perspectives on Service Alternatives

Dimensions	Basic Literacy	Business and Career Information	Commons	Community Referral	Consumer Information
Vision of individual	Active—to improve reading skills	Reactive—to provide specialized information when requested	Active—social and inquiring	Reactive—to provide specific information when requested	Reactive—to provide specific information when requested
Role of users	Dependent	Self-directed	Independent	Dependent	Autonomous
Valued services	Directed services—work with volunteers	Directed services—provide assistance in selecting and finding information	A community center, a gathering place, a place of refuge, a safe place for children	Directed services—knowledge of community resources that have the potential to be of value	Directed services—provide assistance in selecting and finding consumer-related information
Valued resources	Primarily printed materials—specialized materials and software	Chiefly printed reference materials supplemented with access to online databases	Meeting rooms, auditorium, study tables, comfortable chairs for reading	Maintain a database of community resources—governmental, nonprofit, and corporate organizations	Chiefly printed reference materials supplemented with access to online databases
Approach with users	Personalized, one-on-one	Personalized, one-on-one	Passive	Reactive and personalized	Personalized, one-on-one
Purpose of programming	To encourage—an awards ceremony, for example	Inform people about the availability of materials and services	Provide a wide range of programs—lectures, performances, discussions	To information people about the availability of resources	Inform people about the availability of materials and services
Purpose of technology	Diagnostic and useful to improve skills through repetition	Facilitate access to information	Support the programming activities	Maintain a community referral database of organizations	Facilitate access to information

Table 3.4. Perspectives on Service Alternatives (Cont.)

Dimensions	Cultural Awareness	Current Topics and Titles	Support Formal Learning	General Information	Government Information	Information Literacy	Lifelong Learning
Vision of individual	Reactive—to provide specialized information when requested	To give people what they want—passive	To educate—active	Reactive—to provide specialized information when requested	Reactive—to provide specialized information when requested	Active—to improve information management skills	Passive
Role of users	Both independent and dependent	Autonomous	Dependent	Both independent and dependent	Both independent and dependent	Dependent	Independent
Valued services	Self-selected services—use of indexes and materials. Directed services—research assistance	Self-selected services—reservations, best seller lists	Directed services—readers' assistance, reference	Directed services—readers' assistance, reference	Directed services—readers' assistance, access to government documents	Directed services—training classes	Self-selected services—recommended book lists
Valued resources	Local newspaper indexes, local historical materials	Variety of media—books, audio (cassettes, CDs), video (cassettes, DVDs)	Books, reference materials	General reference materials, maps, dictionaries and so forth	Government documents (federal, state, and local)	Generally handouts and exercises	Wide variety of materials—principally books
Approach with users	Self-directed and personalized	Efficient	Personalized	Efficient—length of interaction generally short	Self-directed and personalized	Personalized	Self-directed
Purpose of programming	To promote cultural awareness and provide training	Enticement, way to attract people	Essential to promote books and reading	To information people about the availability of resources	To information people about the availability of resources	To information people about the importance of information management skills	To promote discussion and critical thinking
Purpose of technology	Facilitates access to information	Facilitates service transactions	Facilitates access to information	Facilitates access to information	Facilitates access to information	Use for class exercises and development of skills	Provides access to library resources

Adapted from France Bouthillier. The Meaning of Service: Ambiguities and Dilemmas for Public Library Service Providers. *Library & Information Science Research*, 22, (3), 2000, 262.

- *Segments of the market.* Another approach is to identify specific segments of the population and focus the library's services on that group or groups. Well-known examples of population segments include young children, teenagers, young adults, and senior citizens.

- **Synergy.** The library might explore ways in which its customers can add value so that other library users will benefit:

  - *Enhance customer value.* The library might allow library users to add comments and rate an item in the library's collection, similar to what can be done when visiting Amazon.com. The library might license access to various complementary databases that provide book reviews, images of book covers, biographical information about authors, and so forth.

  - *Reduce operation cost.* The library might wish to explore options that reduce the operational costs for providing a service so that the freed-up funds can be used for another purpose.

To create superior value, two types of knowledge are required: having a clear understanding of what customers value and organizing the library's resources to respond to customer needs.

Table 3.5. The Importance of Various Public Library Roles

Roles	The Public	Opinion Leaders
Formal education support center	88%	88%
Independent learning center	85%	78%
Preschoolers' door to learning	83%	81%
Research center	68%	56%
Community information center	66%	65%
Reference library—business	55%	47%
Reference library—personal	48%	38%
Public workplace	52%	38%
Popular materials library	51%	53%
Community Activities Center	41%	46%

Avoiding some of the more commonly made mistakes will allow the library to move from strategy formulation to implementation with comparative ease. Some of these mistakes are confusing strategies with goals that are derived from the library's vision, not developing the cause-and-effect relationships between strategies and the anticipated goals, failing to identify and implement performance measures that accurately measure the strategy, and not devoting sufficient time and resources to the training and instruction of all employees.[18]

Many books and articles about strategy will mention MOST (mission, objectives, strategy, tactics), an acronym that suggests there is a structure and order to strategy development. Using the organization's mission statement as the starting point, objectives are defined, strategies developed, and short-term tactics agreed upon. Unfortunately the process of developing winning strategies is much more messy, iterative, and normally determined through a trial-and-error process.[19]

> *In a world that is forever changing, the only certainty is change. Therefore, strategies for building the 21st century libraries and librarians must focus on the ability of librarians and libraries to not just adapt to change, but to prepare for it, facilitate it, and shape it.*—Roy Tennant[20]

Specific Library Strategies

The public library has available a number of strategies that can be utilized as it seeks to serve its customers. Some of these strategies involve tradeoffs: The use of one strategy may mean that another strategy cannot be employed. Some of the specific library strategies are described below.

Strategy 1

The size and composition of a library's collection is a very important key strategy. For many, the specific collection-based strategies used by a particular library are what determine the usefulness and value of that library. Does the library follow a strategy emphasizing a large "just-in-case" collection versus a smaller collection that is complemented by a "just-in-time" delivery of information resources using interlibrary loan and document delivery? Is collection defined as only the resources to be found within the library, or is it more broadly defined as providing access to information resources (physical materials + electronic journals + eBooks + selected Web sites) regardless of their location? As the traditional library moves along the continuum to embrace electronic resources, which some have called the digital library or the virtual library; the library becomes a hybrid library.

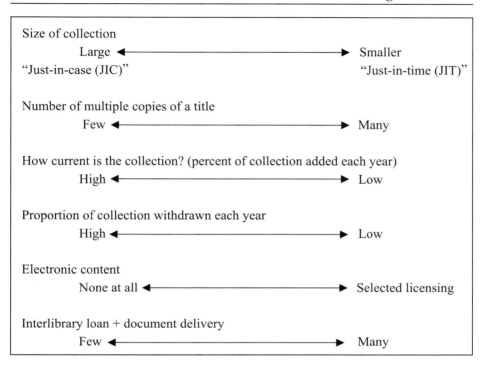

Strategy 2

The library may wish to provide a service, often called an "alert service," that informs customers about the additions to the "collection." Collection may be defined simply as new books or it may be more broadly defined as books plus other material, for example, articles in electronic journals (databases).

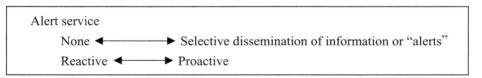

Strategy 3

The public library must determine the number of magazines, journals, and newspapers it will provide in print format as well as whether it will provide access to a database of electronic journals. Would the library provide to interested customers information about the tables of contents of selected journals?

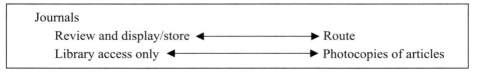

Strategy 4

Providing access to a wide variety of audiovisual materials is another important strategy decision for the public library.

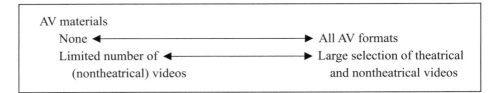

Strategy 5

The role of the library's catalog is yet another important strategy for the library to consider. Among the strategic issues that should be addressed is the role of authority control; whether reviews of materials are provided; whether the library's patrons can add a summary, comments, or a rating; and what information resources are included in the catalog. If records of Internet resources are provided in the library's catalog, are complementary subject guides or pathfinders available (in print and online)?

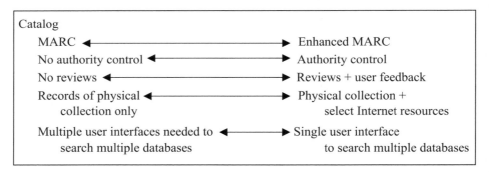

Strategy 6

Does the library provide any assistance to a customer who wants a thorough search done, or are customers on their own?

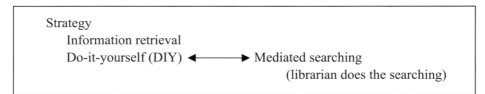

Strategy 7

Providing reference services is a traditional and important service in most public libraries. However, there are several strategies related to reference that must be decided.

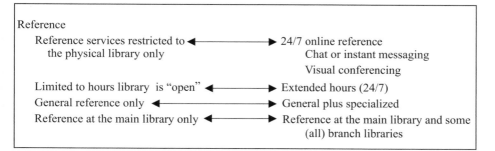

Reference
Reference services restricted to ⟷ 24/7 online reference
   the physical library only   Chat or instant messaging
                   Visual conferencing
Limited to hours library is "open" ⟷ Extended hours (24/7)
General reference only ⟷ General plus specialized
Reference at the main library only ⟷ Reference at the main library and some
                   (all) branch libraries

Strategy 8

The library must determine which activities by library staff members are key or core competencies for the library and which activities might be outsourced. Must all staff members be physically located in the library, or may some work remotely?

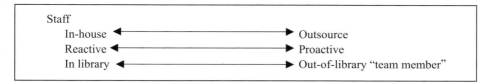

Staff
   In-house ⟷ Outsource
   Reactive ⟷ Proactive
   In library ⟷ Out-of-library "team member"

Strategy 9

Yet another strategy pertaining to library staff members is the role of technical services. Does the technical services team work efficiently (as measured by the turnaround time to process materials once received by the library)? Has the library considered outsourcing the cataloging and processing of new materials to a vendor?

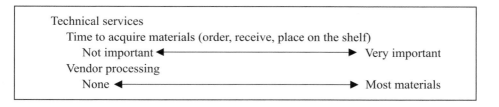

Technical services
   Time to acquire materials (order, receive, place on the shelf)
      Not important ⟷ Very important
   Vendor processing
      None ⟷ Most materials

Strategy 10

The role that information technology will play in providing library services is a crucial strategy for any public library. May a customer find access to the library using a telephone, fax machine, e-mail, library Web site, 24/7 reference services, and so forth? Recent software enhancements and the development of new standards make it possible to deliver a new, more personalized era of service. Does the library view information technology merely as a means of improving staff productivity, or is information technology being used as a tool to facilitate more frequent communication between the user and the library?

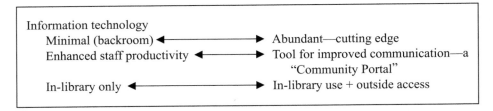

Strategy 11

How many days a week and how many hours per day is the library to be open? Are the open hours appealing or convenient for a large number of customers (number of hours open after normal business hours and weekends)? Are the hours open each week the same at each library facility?

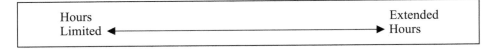

Strategy 12

Does the public library have more than one facility? If there is more than one facility, is there a large "main" library? Are the branch library locations distributed to maximize the number of residents located within three to five miles of each branch library? Are retail store-type locations considered? Generally the most important influence on circulation, community characteristics excepted, is the size of the branch bookstock.[21]

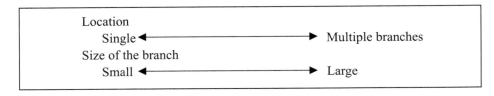

Although these are some of the more important strategies, there are clearly a number of other strategies and approaches for providing service that a public library can choose to follow. The important point is to make sure that the strategies selected lead to fulfilling the library's vision.

The Planning Process

Using as a foundation the knowledge about the various library user segments of the community and their corresponding information needs allows the library to articulate its mission statement. The various factors likely to influence the library and the services it provides are identified and then used to help craft the vision statement. Knowing where the library is currently and where it wants to go, the library then can explore what strategies it wishes to use to move the library toward its vision of the future. And helping to ensure that the library meets its goals, the library chooses a set of performance measures to track over time. An overview of the planning process is shown in Figure 3.7.

> *Plans are worthless: Planning is everything.*—Dwight D. Eisenhower[22]

The important thing about planning is to recognize that it is a process. Planning should not be done every three to five years but as a regular process to learn from previous efforts and to identify new goals and opportunities for improvement. The goal of planning and the use of performance measurement is to help the library to do a better job rather than attempting to assess the "goodness" of the library.

Since a majority of public libraries do not collect performance measures to assist in monitoring the library's progress toward achieving its vision but rather rely on collecting mandated and locally selected operational statistics, the library rarely looks at its performance from a strategic perspective but rather from an operational perspective.

Libraries with an operational perspective are focused on short-term actions, routine ongoing tasks, improving the efficiency of existing operations, and immediately resolving any problems that may occur. In short, the operational perspective is inward focused and the view is short-term and in-the-trenches. An alternative strategic perspective is that of a library that is paying attention to the long-term, is attempting to identify key issues and opportunities, wants to assess the effectiveness of its services, and has a broader view from 10,000 feet. A library adopting the strategic perspective will want to create and maintain a "culture of assessment."

In short, the public library, as a part of its planning process, should be able to answer seven key questions:

- *What* do we do?

- *Who* are we here for?

- What do they *want* and why?

- How can we better *improve* their satisfaction and the library's performance?

- What is the *strategy* and *process* for delivering library services?

- *What* needs to be done? *Who* will do it? *When*?

- Do we know or can we *determine* the library's contribution to the quality of life of a particular community?

Summary

This chapter has noted the importance of the library establishing and publishing the library's mission statement, vision, and values and articulating what strategies it will follow as it seeks to delivery quality library services while moving forward to achieve its vision of the future. The benefit of such an approach is that all of the library's stakeholders, be they library users, interested citizens, staff, or funding decision makers, will have a clear understanding of the library's goals and objectives.

Notes

1. Leah K. Starr. The Future of Public Libraries. *Public Libraries*, 34, March/April 1995, 103.

2. Cited in M. B. Line. What Do People Need of Libraries, and How Can We Find Out? *Australian Academic & Research Libraries, 27, June 1996, 79.*

3. Rebecca Jones. Business Plans: Roadmaps for Growth & Success. *Information Outlook*, 4 (12), December 2000, 22–29.

4. Quoted in John Blagden and John Harrington. *How Good Is Your Library: A Review of Approaches to the Evaluation of Library and Information Services.* London: Aslib, 1990, 46.

5. Nils-Goran Olve, Jan Roy, and Magnus Wetter. *Performance Drivers: A Practical Guide to Using the Balanced Scorecard.* New York: Wiley, 1999.

6. George D'Elia and Eleanor J. Rodger. Public Library Roles and Patron Use: Why Patrons Use the Library. *Public Libraries*, 33 (3), 1994, 135–44.

7. Joan Frye Williams. Shaping the "Experience Library." *American Libraries*, 53 (4), April 2002, 69–72.

8. Thomas Patterson. Idea Stores: London's New Libraries. *Library Journal*, 126 (8), May 1, 2001, 48–49.

9. Simon Wootton and Terry Horne. *Strategic Thinking: A Step-by-Step Approach to Strategy*. Dover, NH: Kogan Page, 2000.

10. Quoted in William A. Schiemann and John H. Lingle. *Bullseye! Hitting Your Strategic Targets Through High-Impact Measurement*. New York: Free Press, 1999, 61.

11. R. Charan and G. Colvin. Why CEOs Fail. *Fortune*, 139, June 21, 1999, 68–78. A similar analysis performed in the early 1980s noted the same result; see Walter Kiechel. Corporate Strategists Under Fire. *Fortune*, 106, December 27, 1982, 34–39.

12. Michael Porter. What Is Strategy? *Harvard Business Review*, 74 (6), November/December 1996, 61–79.

13. Gerry Johnson and Kevan Scholes. Exploring Corporate Strategy. 5th ed. London: Prentice Hall, 1999.

14. Michael Treacy and Fred Wiersema. Customer Intimacy and Other Value Disciplines. *Harvard Business Review*, 71 (1), January/February 1993, 84–93.

15. Ethel Himmel and William James Wilson. *Planning for Results: A Public Library Transformation Process. The Guidebook*. Chicago: American Library Association, 1998.

16. Matthew Simon. Will the Library Survive the Internet? What Patrons Value in Public Libraries. *Public Libraries*, 41 (2), March/April 2002, 104–6.

17. George D'Elia and Eleanor J. Rodger. Public Opinion about the Roles of the Public Library in the Community: The Results of a Recent Gallup Poll. *Public Libraries*, 33 (1), January/February 1994, 23–28; George D'Elia and Eleanor J. Rodger. The Roles of the Public Library in the Community: The Results of a Gallup Poll of Community Opinion Leaders. *Public Libraries*, 34, March/April 1995, 94–101.

18. Heather Johnson. Strategic Planning for Modern Libraries. *Library Management*, 15 (1), 1994, 7–18.

19. Andrew Campbell and Marcus Alexander. What's Wrong with Strategy? *Harvard Business Review*, 75 (6), November–December 1997, 42–51.

20. Roy Tennant. Strategies for Building 21st Century Libraries and Librarians, in *Robots to Knowbots: The Wider Automation Agenda. Proceedings of the Victorian Association for Library Automation 9th Biennial Conference, January 28–30, 1998*. Melbourne: VALA, 1998, 503–7.

21. Robert E. Couglin et al. *Urban Analysis for Branch Library System Planning*. Westport, CT: Greenwood, 1972.

22. Speech given to the National Defense Executive Resource Conference at the Department of Commerce, Washington, D.C., on November 14, 1957.

Public Library Users

Despite the excess of research about public library users, only sketchy information is available about the reasons why people do, and do not, use their local library.[2] This chapter is organized around three themes: the user, use of the library, and uses or purposes of a visit to the public library. Douglas Zweizig and Brenda Dervin first articulated the need to shift the focus of research from identifying the users of the library, or quantifying the amount of library use, to exploring how the library is used.[3]

The User

Among the many published studies of public library users and the many more unpublished reports prepared by library staff and consultants, several consistent public library user characteristics emerge. The characteristics most frequently examined in these studies are sex, age, education, family income, marital status, and the number of small children living at home.

Carol Kronus prepared an analysis that determined what variables explained some part of the use of the public library.[4] Her analysis suggested that education, urban residence, and family life cycle factors predicted rate of library use. The commonly used factors of age, sex, and race had no independent influence on library use.

Attempting to better understand the relationships between library use and user characteristics, George D'Elia developed a model with a hierarchy of variables that included such items as individual characteristics, patron awareness of library services, perceived accessibility, and ease of library use.[5] He concluded that users of the public library perceived the library as more accessible than nonusers and that frequency and intensity of use were related to awareness of the range of available library services.

Ronald Powell, looking for a more predictive answer concerning library use, examined the personality of the user. He found no link between personality type and use of the library.[6]

A recent survey conducted on behalf of the American Library Association indicated that about 62 percent of Americans have a library card.[7] Thus, demographics partially predict who will use the library and who will not. Other nondemographic factors such as lifestyle, social roles, and travel distance also influence library use. A combination of demographic factors is often more important than a single characteristic. The characteristics of the public library user that have been discussed and analyzed in a large number of user studies include:

- **Education**. The more education individuals receive, the more likely they are to use the public library. Education is the single most important predictor of library use, and it is not unusual for more than half of library users to have some college education, a college degree, or postgraduate work.[8] Although it is true that income, occupation, and education are all inter-correlated, regression analysis demonstrates that everything disappears except education.

- **Age**. There is consistent evidence suggesting that those who use the library the most are young adults and that use of the library declines with age. However, Kronus noted that the relationship between public library use and age was misleading and not statistically valid. Library users in 2002 were[9]

Age	Percent
18–24	14
25–34	19
35–44	23
45–54	17
55 +	21

- **Number of small children**. Adults with small children are more likely to have a library card and to visit the library on a fairly regular basis (the greater the number of children the more frequently the library is used). Households with children are much more likely to use the public library than those without children—61 percent compared to 35 percent.[10]

- **Family income**. Individuals with higher incomes will use the local library more frequently. However, use is greater among middle income levels than among the poor or the rich. It may be that low use of the library by the poor may be related to poor reading skills. In 2002, a quarter of library user households earned from $25,000 to $49,999, while more than one-third earned $50,000 or more.[11] Similar results were noted in a 1991 survey showing that use of the public library was clearly correlated with family income.[12] With increased income comes discretionary time for reading and information- seeking activities.

  One study found that higher incomes tended to be associated with higher library usage rates per capita using a "library activity" index composed of circulation, in-library use of materials, number of reference transactions, and annual program attendance.[13] This study also noted that other factors will affect the use of library services, including the availability and location of branch libraries, number of hours open, and size and scope of the library's collection.

- **Sex**. Women are more prone to use the library than men, although Bernard Berelson noted that men use reference services more frequently while women use circulation services more than men. Although women use the library more than men, taking employment status into consideration and holding education constant, the dominant use by women disappears.[14]

- **Marital status**. Single individuals use the library more than married people. This is likely the case since single adults are younger than married adults, and use declines with age. In addition, married adults probably have less leisure time than single adults due to domestic responsibilities.

- **Ethnicity**. Depending on the ethnic population within a community, use of the library will generally reflect the relative proportions of the population, although more use will likely occur among members of the white ethnic group. One national survey found that 56 percent of users were white, while 38 and 42 percent of the respondents were Hispanic and black respectively.[15] Another more recent national survey found that among households that had used a public library, 80 percent were white, 9 percent black, and 7 percent Hispanic, which is roughly representative of the distribution of the U.S. population.[16]

  One study found that patrons of color use the library for educational support and for information gathering more than do their Caucasian counterparts.[17]

  Racial and ethnic minority groups are growing at a much faster pace than the general U.S. population. Therefore, a public library should periodically review the demographic shifts that are occurring within its geographic and service area boundaries.

Using a geographic information system (GIS), Christine Koontz mapped demographic and library use data for several public libraries with branches, finding that branch libraries serving primarily minority populations had higher in-library use, more reference transactions, and greater program attendance while at the same time having lower circulation figures.[18] This is significant since most public library systems will often use circulation as the sole indicator of a branch library's performance.

As the demographics of many communities continue to change, traditional minority groups are growing numerically and in political power. Some public libraries will need to assess whether their traditional library services, provided in the majority of branch libraries, are the right mix of services for this underserved population.

Segmenting Users

Historically, marketing has segmented markets using a geographic basis or by employing user demographics, as noted above. A third approach is to identify segments based on volume of use of library services. A fourth approach is to use benefit segmentation: to identify market segments by causal factors rather than descriptive ones. That is, the benefits sought by users of the library will shape their behavior much more accurately than other approaches to market segmentation.[19] It is important to understand that more frequent or heavy users of the public library will have different needs and benefit expectations than do infrequent library users. Thus it would seem important to understand the benefits that different groups of library users are searching for.

One study found that people with an information need in either work or nonwork situations consulted a public library only 17 percent of the time. People were more likely to consult with other people or institutions, and the public library was near the bottom of the list.[20]

What Is in a Name?

There are many words to describe the individual who visits or uses the library and its resources, including the following:

- *Customers* emphasizes that individuals have a choice when they "purchase" a library service. The use of the word customer is proactive and stresses the service context of the public library experience.

- *Clients* stresses a relationship between a user and a professional adviser that delivers a high level of personal service. The word client is rarely used in the public library context.

- *Patrons* emphasizes the fact that users are supporting the library through their use of the collection and the library's services.

- *Readers* suggests that the primary purpose of the library is to provide reading materials and a place to read them. The use of the term reader occurs infrequently in U.S. public libraries.

- *Card holders,* or registered borrowers, emphasizes that although many people could have obtained a library card, only a subset will actually be users of the library.

- *Borrowers* suggests that the library is in business for the principal purpose of loaning materials (and may or may not provide remote access services or access to electronic resources).

- *Users* implies people who are already using the library. In fact, users are those who have learned to adjust to the layout, services, and systems found in the local library.

So is a registered borrower or library cardholder a user? In some cases, yes. It really depends on how frequently that person actually uses a library; use of the library at least once a month has long been considered a measure of the "real user."[21] The relationship between the user and the library is complex and changing, and for the purposes of this book, the terms *user* and *customer* are used interchangeably.

Nonusers

Public libraries are reluctant to admit that they will never serve 100 percent of their citizens. Some people, for a variety of reasons, don't know what or where the library is, wouldn't know how to find information once they arrived at a library, or place little emphasis on reading or on other information services normally found at the local public library and thus will never obtain a public library card. Part of the planning process should be to recognize what proportion of the population "might" be interested in public library services and then determine how the library is doing in terms of meeting the needs of "prospective users." Figure 4.1 (page 62) illustrates the various components of the residents who make up the total potential service population.

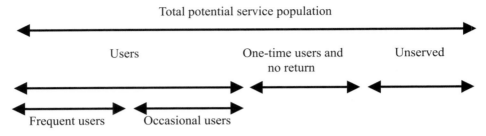

Figure 4.1. Users and Potential User Populations

Interestingly, most public libraries do very little to figure out why someone will come once to the library, obtain a library card, and then never return. A library could use a brief mail survey, a focus group, or other means to identify the reasons why people don't return to the library. A survey of former library users in Jefferson County, Colorado (located just west of Denver) who had not used the library in more than a year revealed that the typical "once but no-longer a user" was an employed (one-third were retired), well-educated Caucasian over the age of 50.[22] In short, the typical no-longer users were "empty nesters" who either were too busy or would rather buy books than visit the local public library.

Remember that while consumers can have a major impact on a retail store by refusing to buy, few public libraries are affected when a single user or even large numbers of "once-but-no-longer users" decline to return to the library.

Use of the Library

The decision of an individual to use the public library, according to Maurice Marchant, occurs when the user's motivation is stronger than the inhibitions that discourage use.[23] Four specific motivators were examined, and Marchant found that all four—home and family life, vocational growth, religion, and politics—led to use of the public library.

Among the many possible inhibitors of use of the library are inadequate or inconvenient hours of service, inadequate library collection, inconvenient library location, lack of parking, lack of library skills, competing demands for time during nonwork hours of the day, poor health, lack of transportation, and so forth. Despite the inhibitors, the public library remains a popular destination for a great many individuals within a community.

Frequency of Visits

Depending on the community and characteristics of its population, public library users in 2002 visited the library: [24]

Weekly	14%
Twice a month	11%
Monthly	9%
Less than once a month	31%

A national survey conducted in 1991 found that 21 percent of respondents had used the public library in the past year and another 32 percent in the past month.[25] These findings are somewhat in conflict with the results of more recent surveys. A U.S. News/CNN poll found that 67 percent of adults had gone to a library at least once in the past year.[26] And a 1996 survey conducted by the U.S. Department of Education found that 44 percent of individuals had used the library in the last month, and a total of 65 percent had used the public library in the last year.[27] Results were similar in a Gallup that poll found that 66 percent of Americans had used a public library at least once in the past year.[28] A more recent national survey found that 46 percent had used a public library within the last six months and that a total of 57 percent had visited the library in the last year.[29]

Summarizing the results of a number of user studies, Douglas Zweizig and Brenda Dervin noted that on average, 20 percent of adults use the public library at least once a month.[30] Thus, a fairly small proportion of users will account for most visits to the library. This statistical phenomenon is known as the normal Pareto distribution. That is, a relatively small number of users (20 percent) will account for 80 percent of the visits to the library. This same Pareto principle will also apply to circulation of library materials.

Location of the User

The vast majority of people visiting a public library, especially a branch library, live within a few miles of the library facility. Christine Koontz, summarizing the research in this area, noted that some 57 percent of users live within two miles, 27 percent live within two to four miles, and 5 percent live within five miles of a public library.[31]

In general, library usage falls off rapidly with distance. Urban residents who wish to walk to their local library prefer smaller libraries.[32] Since library facilities typically are designed to last 25 years or longer, locating a facility in other than the "best" site will result in lack of access and reduced use, which means diminished efficiency and effectiveness. In a study that examined demographic, spatial, quality of the library, and library use variables, Koontz found that demographic variables alone do not accurately predict library use, but topographical features, hours of operation, size of the building, and unique population characteristics do affect library use.[33] In short, the factors that matter to the location of fire stations, retail stores, and other important facilities where time to travel to a specific location is important are also essential, or should be key, to libraries. However, when people have developed the library "habit," they will travel farther to obtain more or better materials.[34]

Uses of the Library

Acknowledged experts on users and how they use libraries, Brenda Dervin and Benson Fraser documented 16 benefits or "helps" by tracking what people did with information and attempting to determine what was the "end result."[35] They felt that information was a "means to an end" and that a better understanding of the transition of means to ends would be helpful as libraries planned for the future. Among their "helps" were that users

- found direction, reached goals, or got skills;
- felt connected;
- got ideas/understanding;
- got happiness/pleasure; and
- got support/emotional control.

Dervin and Fraser noted that people who visited public libraries were much more likely to experience "happiness/pleasure" than those who visited other types of libraries. It is also important to be realistic about how people look for information. More often than not, people will check the Internet; ask a friend, relative, or knowledgeable person (doctor, lawyer, nurse, or minister), or consult a newspaper, magazine, or television before thinking to turn to a public library.[36]

In a study of Pennsylvania public libraries, Charles McClure and John Bertot found that libraries play an important role in the everyday lives of people.[37] Their report is filled with anecdotes that illustrate the qualitative impact public libraries have. A similar study in England found that: public libraries support education, careers, job training, and literacy; are a cohesive force within a community by supporting special groups, for example, seniors; and foster community pride.[38]

A nationwide U.S. survey discovered that public libraries had a positive impact on the quality of life (51 percent) and improved the lives of the respondents (41 percent).[39] Of those who felt that the local library had improved their lives, a large majority felt that the library provided educational enrichment, improved their reading skills, or provided entertainment.

The purposes of library use vary throughout life. Use for recreational purposes increases with age, while access to information resources is more important to younger people and declines with age.[40] Depending on the community, the largest single category of use of the public library is either recreational reading or educational purposes.[41]

A 2002 ALA-funded survey found that adults go to the local public library for a number of reasons, as shown in Table 4.1. If the survey had included both children and adults, the results would likely be different.

Table 4.1. Use of American Public Libraries

Rank	Reason	Percent of Visits for That Reason
1	Borrow books	67
2	Use reference materials	47
3	Consult the librarian	47
4	Read newspapers or magazines	31
5	Connect to the Internet/e-mail	26
6	Take out CDs, videos, or computer software	25
7	Hear a speaker, see a movie, attend a special event	14

Adapted from KRC Research & Consulting. @ *Your Library.* See also Vavrek,
Is the American Public Library Part of Everyone's Life?

An earlier study found similar reasons for visiting the local public library, as shown in Table 4.2.

Table 4.2. Purpose of Public Library Visit

Rank	Reason
1	For enjoyment or hobbies, including to borrow books or tapes or to attend activities
2	To get information for personal use such as consumer or health issues, investments, and so on
3	For a school or class assignment
4	For a work assignment or to keep up to date at work
5	To get information to help find a job
6	For a program or activity designed for children ages six to twelve
7	For an activity for children under six, such as story hour, or other introduction to books and reading
8	To work with a tutor or take a class to learn to read

Adapted from Mary Jo Lynch. Using Public Libraries: What Makes a Difference?
American Libraries, 28 (10), November 1997, 64–65.

When people use the Internet, some 65 percent do so "for enjoyment or hobbies," 57 percent to "get information for personal use," 53 percent "for a school assignment," 35 percent "for a work assignment or to keep up to date at work," and 27 percent "to help find a job."[42]

> *Public librarians must stop confusing the most*
> *commonly occurring activity in the public library*
> *(leisure reading) with the most important activity*
> *of the public library (lifelong learning). Counts*
> *and accountability are not synonymous.*—Kenneth Shearer[43]

A study employing portable data scanners collected information about in-library use of services and materials in a wide range of urban, suburban, and rural public libraries.[44] An analysis of the data indicated that in-library use of materials and services is larger than annual circulation figures, the demographics of library users play an important role in materials selected and desired, and such knowledge of actual use by minority populations can assist in designing library facilities to better accommodate likely behavior. For example, Hispanic users tend to be younger than other minority groups, and math and science subject areas have the highest in-library use by juveniles. In addition, computer usage is highest among juveniles and young adults, and the Internet and e-mail represent the primary use of the computer.

One study conducted in England during 1999 identified the wide variety of reasons for visiting a local public library, as shown in Table 4.3. Six of the top ten reasons were focused on the use of the library's collection. Although use of the Internet ranked eighteenth during this time period, it would be likely that the use of Internet would receive a higher ranking today. In addition, the size and breadth of the library's resources in a particular area, for example videotapes, will have an impact on the popularity of any particular resource.

Table 4.3. Use of Public Libraries in England

Rank	Purpose	Central Libraries Percent of Visits for	Branch Libraries Percent of Visits for	Rank
1	Borrow/return/ renew books	62	65	1
2	Use reference books	33	16	2
3	Study and work	27	7	8
4	Ask for information	17	11	4

(Continued)

Table 4.3. Use of Public Libraries in England (*Cont.*)

Rank	Purpose	Central Libraries Percent of Visits for	Branch Libraries Percent of Visits for	Rank
5	Borrow/return/ renew CDs	14	6	12
6	User reference journals	12	3	14
7	Use the photocopier	12	9	6
8	Read newspapers	12	7	10
9	Consult the library catalog	11	6	11
10	Borrow/return/ renew audiotapes	11	8	7
11	Borrow/return/ renew videotapes	10	14	3
12	Meet friends	7	2	16
13	Use for another family member	7	10	5
14	Make a reservation	7	7	9
15	Use the archives	6	3	13
16	Borrow/return/ renew journals	4	2	15
17	Use CD-ROMs (databases)	3	1	18
18	Use the Internet	2	1	18
19	Use word processing computers	1	1	20
20	Use online databases	1	1	21
21	Use open learning materials	1	1	17

Adapted from C. Nankivell, W. Foster, and J. Elkin. *People Flows*.
London: Library and Information Commission, 1999.

Australian public library users came to the library for the following reasons: recreational reading or hobby (42 percent), study (23 percent), visiting on behalf of children or teenagers (13 percent), and job- or career-related purposes (5 percent).[45] Thus, it would seem that public library users from around the world come to the library for similar reasons.

Another English study asked respondents to identify their reasons for borrowing nonfiction books from the public library. The most popular reason was that the individual was seeking some practical information, followed by reading for pleasure, as noted in Table 4.4. The usefulness of information contained within these books was judged by the library users to be quite high.

Table 4.4. Reasons for Borrowing Adult Nonfiction

Reason	Percent
Practical information	42
Pleasure	33
Personal growth/learning	30
Education/course of study	29
Hobby	26
Job	10

Adapted from Anne Morris, Margaret Hawkins, and John Sumsion. Value of Book Borrowing from Public Libraries: User Perceptions. *Journal of Librarianship and Information Science*, 33 (4), December 2001, 191–98.

Chandra Prabha, in a study examining the use of nonfiction books, found that people were looking for specific information or information in roughly defined areas. Eighty-four percent of the users reported they found the information they were seeking and expected to use the information within a month.[46] Prabha divided the users of nonfiction books into four groups:

- *True browsers* (26 percent). Books were selected from the shelves, and the individual was not looking for specific information and read all or a part of the book.

- *Information-seeking browsers* (18 percent). Books were selected from the shelves, and the individual was looking for and found specific information and read all or a part of the book.

- *Known-item users* (13 percent). These users had prior knowledge of the book and found the information they were looking for.

- *Information-seeking catalog users* (12 percent). These individuals used the library catalog to select a book, read all or part of the book, and found the information they were seeking.

Nonavailability of the Public Library

Public libraries have become such a part of most people's lives that the thought of a public library closing, for whatever reason, is anathema to most people. For people who use the library there is no substitute. One study in England that examined the impact of the closing of public libraries due to a strike determined that although nine out of ten users missed the library, only 9 percent replaced their library use with nonlibrary-oriented activities.[47] Although almost one-half of the respondents replaced library service with a related activity, they felt that the alternative was not acceptable or satisfactory on a long-term basis. The local bookstores did notice an unexpected increase in sales during the time the libraries were closed.

A related study in England focused on the impact of public library closures and reductions in open hours in 1996–1997. Depending on the locale and the availability of other nearby libraries, between 8 and 29 percent of users lost access to library services (the loss was higher among school children).[48] Not surprisingly, the impact of reduced open hours was less than the impact when the local public library actually shut its doors. Eighty-two percent of the users were able to shift their use of the library to a nearby location that remained open.

Summary

It is clear that the socioeconomic status of the surrounding population is the most important factor in determining how much use will be made of the public library. Those with higher educational achievements and students will use the library more than those with less schooling. Use declines with age, yet when doing a careful statistical analysis, the sole determining factor of library use would seem to be that of educational achievement. In addition, physical distance from the closest public library location also has an impact on the amount of use.

In some communities, the demographics of neighborhoods are changing, in some cases radically. Thus public libraries, especially those with branch facilities, should reexamine the mix of services, collections, and staff to deliver the most effective services to the surrounding community.

Notes

1. Don Revill. The Measurement of Performance, in J. Cowley (Ed.). *The Management of Polytechnic Libraries*. London: Gower, 1985, 132.

2. Ronald R. Powell. Library Use and Personality: The Relationship Locus of Control and Frequency of Use. *Library and Information Science Research*, 6, 1984, 179–90.

3. Douglas L. Zweizig. With Our Eye on the User: Needed Research for Information and Referral in the Public Library. *Drexel Library Quarterly*, 12, 1976, 48–58; Douglas L. Zweizig. Measuring Library Use. *Drexel Library Quarterly*, 13, 1977, 3–15; Douglas Zweizig and Brenda Dervin. Public Library Use, Users, and Uses: Advances in Knowledge of the Characteristics and Needs of the Adult Clientele of American Public Libraries. *Advances in Librarianship*, 7, 1977, 232–57; Brenda Dervin. Useful Theory for Librarianship: Communication, Not Information. *Drexel Library Quarterly*, 13 (3), July 1977, 16–32.

4. Carol I. Kronus. Patterns of Adult Library Use: A Regression and Path Analysis. *Adult Education*, 23, 1973, 115–31.

5. George D'Elia. The Development and Testing of a Conceptual Model of Public Library User Behavior. *Library Quarterly*, 50, 1980, 410–30.

6. Powell. Library Use and Personality, 179–90.

7. KRC Research & Consulting. *@ Your Library: Attitudes Toward Public Libraries Survey*. June 2002. Available at: http://www.ala.org/pio/presskits/nlw2002kit/krc_data.pdf (accessed June 16, 2003).

8. Unless otherwise noted, the summary of the user characteristics is based on a review of the work of Berelson, Kronus, and D'Elia in Ronald R. Powell. *The Relationship of Library User Studies to Performance Measures: A Review of the Literature*. Occasional Paper Number 181. Champaign: University of Illinois, Graduate School of Library and Information Science, 1988.

9. KRC Research & Consulting, *@ Your Library*.

10. Mary Jo Lynch. Using Public Libraries: What Makes a Difference? *American Libraries*, 28 (10), November 1997, 64–65.

11. KRC Research & Consulting, *@ Your Library*.

12. Jim Scheppke. Who's Using the Public Library. *Library Journal*, 119, October 15, 1994, 35–37.

13. Mary Kopczynski and Michael Lombardo. Comparative Performance Measurement: Insights and Lessons Learned from a Consortium Effort. *Public Administration Review*, 59 (2), March/April 1999, 124–34.

14. Kronus, Patterns of Adult Library Use.

15. Scheppke. Who's Using the Public Library.

16. Lynch. Using Public Libraries.

17. Geore D'Elia and Eleanor J. Rodger. Public Library Roles and Patron Use: Why Patrons Use the Library. *Public Libraries*, 33 (3), 1994, 135–44.

18. Christine M. Koontz. Technology—Pied Piper or Playground Bully, or Creating Meaningful Measures Using Emerging Technologies: Separating the Reality from the Myths. *Proceedings of the 4th Northumbria International Conference on Performance Measurement & Libraries & Information Services*. New Castle, England: University of Northumbria, 2001.

19. R. I. Haley. Benefit Segmentation: A Decision Oriented Research Tool. *Journal of Marketing*, 32, July 1968, 30–35.

20. Ching-chih Chen and Peter Hernon. Library Effectiveness in Meeting Information Consumer's Needs, in *Library Effectiveness: A State of the Art. Papers from a 1980 ALA Preconference, June 27 & 28, 1980, New York, NY.* Chicago: American Library Association, 1980, 49–63.

21. Zweizig and Dervin. Public Library Use, Users, and Uses.

22. Kathy L. Harris. Who Are They? In Search of the Elusive Non-User. *Colorado Libraries*, 27 (4), Winter 2001, 16–18.

23. Maurice P. Marchant. What Motivates Adult Use of Public Libraries? *Library and Information Science Research*, 13, 1991, 201–35.

24. KRC Research & Consulting, @ *Your Library*.

25. Scheppke. Who's Using the Public Library.

26. U.S. News and World Report. More Americans Visit Their Public Library Today Than They Did in 1978. (Press Release). New York: U.S. News and World Report, December 2, 1995.

27. Mary A. Collins and Kathryn Chandler. *Use of Public Library Services by Households in the United States: 1996*. NCES 97-446. Washington, DC: U.S. Department of Education, Office of Educational Research and Improvement, 1997.

28. American Library Association New Gallup Poll Shows Two of Three Adults Are Library Users. (Press Release). *The Unabashed Librarian*, 107, 1998, 8.

29. B. F. Vavrek. Is the American Public Library Part of Everyone's Life? *American Libraries*, 31 (1), 2000, 60–64.

30. Zweizig and Dervin. Public Library Use, Users, and Uses.

31. Christine M. Koontz. *Library Facility Siting and Location Handbook*. Westport, CT: Greenwood, 1997.

32. E. Susan Palmer. The Effect of Distance on Public Library Use: A Literature Survey. *Library Research*, 3, Winter 1981, 315–54.

33. Christine M. Koontz. Public Library Site Evaluation and Location: Past and Present Market-Based Modeling Tools for the Future. *Library and Information Science Research*, 14 (4), 1992, 379–409.

34. Alicia J. Welch and Christine N. Donohue. Awareness, Use, and Satisfaction with Public Libraries. *Public Libraries*, 33 (4), May/June 1994, 149–52.

35. Brenda Dervin and Benson Fraser. *How Libraries Help*. Stockton, CA: University of the Pacific, 1985.

36. Glen E. Holt. Balancing Buildings, Books, Bytes, and Bucks: Steps to Secure the Public Library Future in the Internet Age. *Library Trends*, 46 (1), Summer 1997, 92–116.

37. Charles R. McClure and John Carlo Bertot. *Public Library Use in Pennsylvania: Identifying Uses, Benefits, and Impacts—Final Report*. Harrisburg: Pennsylvania Department of Education, Office of Commonwealth Libraries, 1998. ERIC ED419548

38. Bob Usherwood and Rebecca Linley. New Library—New Measures: A Social Audit of Public Libraries. *IFLA Journal*, 25 (2), 1999, 90–99.

39. Vavrek. Is the American Public Library Part of Everyone's Life?

40. Patrick Timperley and David Spiller. *The Impact of Non-fiction Lending Through Public Libraries*. Loughborough, England: Loughborough University, Library and Information Statistics Unit, 1999.

41. Nicolle O. Steffan, Keith Curry Lance, and Rochelle Logan. Time to Tell the Whole Story: Outcome-Based Evaluation and the Counting on Results Project. *Public Libraries*, July/August 2002, 222–28.

42. Vavrek, Is the American Public Library Part of Everyone's Life?

43. Kenneth Shearer. Confusing What Is Most Wanted with What Is Most Used: A Crisis in Public Library Priorities Today. *Public Libraries*, 32, 1993, 193–97.

44. Dean K. Jue, Christine M. Koontz, and Keith Curry Lance. Collecting Detailed In-library Usage Data in the U.S. Public Libraries: The Methodology, the Results and the Impact, in *Proceedings of the 3rd Northumbria International Conference on Performance Measurement & Libraries & Information Services*. New Castle, England: University of Northumbria, 1999, 175–79.

45. Marina Garlick. Measuring Customer Satisfaction: Myth Or Reality? *Australasian Public Libraries and Information Services,* 11 (2), June 1998, 61–74.

46. Chandra Prabha. *How Public Library Patrons Use Nonfiction Books*. Report Number OCLC/OPR/RR-87/1. Dublin, OH: OCLC, 1987.

47. Richard Proctor, Bob Usherwood, and Gill Sobezyk. *What Do People Do When Their Public Library Service Closes Down? An Investigation into the Impact of the Sheffield Libraries Strike*. British Library R & D Report 6224. London: British Library, 1996.

48. Richard Proctor, Hazel Lee, and Rachel Reilly. *Access to Public Libraries: The Impact of Opening Hours Reductions and Closures 1986–1997*. British Library Research and Innovation Report 90. London: British Library, 1998.

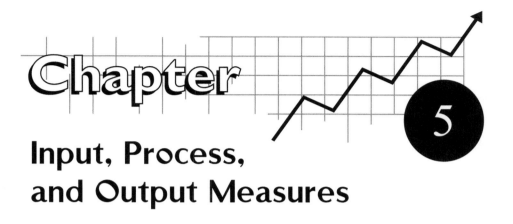

Chapter 5

Input, Process, and Output Measures

Carefully selected and intelligently used, performance measures are perhaps the most important tool the library has to ensure that goals and objectives are being accomplished, to set priorities for resource allocation, to justify services and demonstrate accountability to outside funding agencies, and to identify and set priorities for areas of library activities that require attention.—Robert Swisher and Charles R. McClure[1]

An overabundance of input, process, and output measures is available for a public library to use. Given that the population of potential measures is quite large, what set of measures should a library choose? This chapter explores the strengths and limitations of these three popular types of measures. And while it is possible to evaluate a specific library service, the intention of this book is to focus on evaluating the totality of library services.

A distinction can be made between a performance measure and a performance indicator. A performance measure is something that can be measured directly, for example, a count of circulation checkouts. A performance indicator, on the other hand, is defined as something that must be calculated, such as circulation per capita. Measures are a benchmark for many things. Measures and indicators can tell us *where we have been*, *where we are*, and in what direction *we are heading*. Intelligent use of measures can guide our decisions and assist us in making meaningful comparisons. Measurement relies on the collection and analysis of data, which are then compared to certain yardsticks, such as standards, goals, objectives, and other similar libraries. Performance measures and indicators only inform, they do not prescribe solutions to problems.

Each year, a public library is provided with a set of *resources*. Those resources are organized and directed so that they have the *capability* to provide a set of services. These capabilities are then used. Once used, the information service that has been provided has the potential for a positive, beneficial *impact or effect* on the community.

The relationship among these variables is shown in see Figure 5.1. Figure 5.2 presents the same information from a slightly different perspective to indicate the relationship between quality and value and the fact that the library (the organization) is influenced and constrained by its external environment. Such outside environmental factors include the characteristics of its service population, dependence on an outside organization for financial and other resources, and so forth

Input measures are the easiest to quantify and gather and have been used by librarians for a long time. Librarians will speak of the size of their annual budget, number of professional staff, size of the collection, and so forth. All of these are examples of input measures of the resources provided by the citizens of the community through their taxes.

Process measures focus on the activities that transform resources into services offered by the library and as such are internally directed. Process measures are reflected in an analysis that will quantify the cost or time to perform a specific task or activity. Process measures are ultimately about efficiency and thus answer the question, "Are we doing *things* right?"

Output measures are used to indicate the degree to which the library and its services are being utilized. More often than not, output measures are simply counts to indicate volume of activity. Historically, use of output measures has been regarded as measures of goodness—after all, the library's collection and its services were being used, often intensively so! Therefore, the library was doing "good."

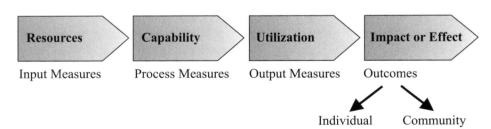

Figure 5.1. Evaluation Model

It should be noted that this model ignores the costs associated with building physical facilities and infrastructure. The financial resources required to create inviting public library facilities are not insignificant. Similarly, additional resources are required, which are reflected in part in the above model, to create a library's collection.

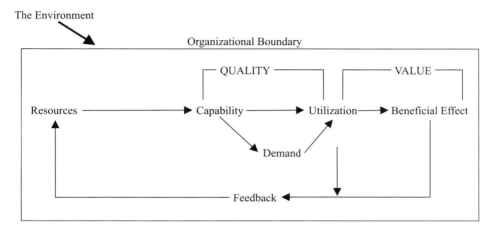

Figure 5.2. Evaluation Model

Input Measures

Input measures indicate the resources that are provided to support the operation of the library. Libraries have traditionally used input measures as performance indicators since they are easy to collect and report. Input measures answer such questions as how much and how many? Another name for an input measure is a *capacity* or *potential* measure. A potential measure describes the ability of the public library to provide access to the library's collection or use a service—for example, the number of Internet workstations.

When considering input measures or the resources available to a library, especially in comparison to other comparable libraries, there often is an implied causal connection between the resources provided and the quality or "goodness" of library services.

Since the 1930s, librarians have been involved in establishing projective standards for public libraries.[2] The objective of qualitative or projective standards is to provide guidelines for the development of library services. However, these "library standards" were immediately beset by controversy and were often considered to be unenforceable guidelines or objectives, even within the professional library community. These library standards were primarily made up of input measures that focused on budgets, staffing, space, size of collection, and so forth.

Standards, used in all sectors of the economy, are the set of specifications or criteria used to measure the quality, shape, or other characteristics of a specific product, process or service. An effective standard is not open to interpretation or variance.[3] Clearly the "projective library standards" were not objective and thus failed even the most generous definition of a "standard." These projective library standards were criticized because:[4]

- The choice of measures and the establishment of threshold values were arbitrary. Phrases such as "generalizations," "vague and wordy," "recommended practices and not standards," "guidelines or a checklist," and "reference points" were used by some to describe and criticize the library standards.

- Some measures were descriptive and subjective, making evaluation difficult.

- They failed to recognize unique characteristics of a user population.

- They focused on input measures.

- The measures were self-serving.

- And, perhaps most important, they offered little leverage in helping a library director to demonstrate shortcomings and obtain additional financial and other resources because they did not offer a persuasive method to demonstrate value for money.[5]

Notwithstanding the number of attempts to produce public library standards, the library profession has moved to the more important question of attempting to identify the outputs of the library. In fact, input measures are a poor measure of performance.

The planning process suggested by the Public Library Association starts with an assessment of the community's needs. The library then chooses a service response(s) of what a library offers to the public in an effort to meet specific community needs, as shown in Figure 5.3. The library then sets goals or targets for the outcomes associated with each service response, establishes short-term objectives for meeting the goals, and decides whether specific projects or activities will be needed to assist in meeting the goals of the library. The planning process recommends use of three types of measures: first, number of people served; second, users' opinions about how well the service met their needs; and third, the number of service units or transactions (output measures). Note that there is no mention of the need to use outcome measures.

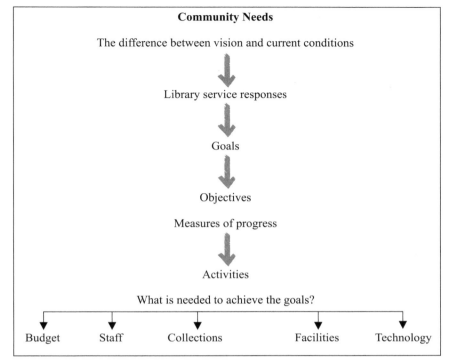

Figure 5.3. The Planning Process

Types of Input Measures

The environment within which a particular public library exists clearly has an impact on the library itself. These environmental constraints are focused most clearly on the library's budget and how the library relates to city or county government or reports to the citizens through the agency of a special district. There are five broad categories of input measures:

- **Income and expenditures**. Measures in this category focus on the library's finances. Knowing the total expenditures in conjunction with other budget-related input measures can supply additional perspectives and insights and allow for comparison with other public libraries. Some commonly used input measures are

  - total income of the library,

  - budget expenditures per capita,

  - budget expenditures per library customer, and

  - budget expenditures for acquisitions (dollars and percent).

- **Staff**. Providing the library with a budget allows it to hire staff and provide services. Among staff-related input measures are

  - total library staff (full-time equivalent or FTE),
  - total library staff (FTE) per capita,
  - total number of librarians (FTE),
  - number of librarians per 1,000 population served,
  - total number of other staff, and
  - number of actual library clients per librarian.

- **Collection**. The public library collection contains materials in a variety of formats. Collection input measures include

  - size of collection—number of titles;
  - size of collection—number of volumes;
  - size of collection (number of volumes) per capita;
  - size of the collection—by subject area, call number range;
  - net growth rate of the collection—percent of titles, volumes; and
  - growth of the collection—number of titles, volumes.

- **Library information system**. An automated library information system is an important asset since access to network infrastructure and a variety of information resources is no longer considered optional. Measures in this area include

  - total dollars spent on the maintenance of the automated system (dollars to the vendor plus staff costs),
  - annual automated system maintenance costs as a percent of the total library's budget,
  - number of staff workstations,
  - number of online catalog workstations (in the library),
  - speed of network connection for each workstation in the library,
  - speed of connection to the branches, and
  - speed of connection to the Internet.

- **Space**. The amount of space provided for shelving the library's collection, staff offices, and other resources plus public service areas is an input measure. Space-related input measures are

  - total space—square feet and
  - space per capita.

The primary problem with input measures is that they provide information about the library without any context, for example, the size of the library's budget, its staff, or its collection. But without some point of reference, that is, compared to other similar libraries, the information is meaningless. The more frequently used input measures are shown in Appendix A.

Process Measures

Process or efficiency measures, sometimes called staff productivity measures, answer the question, "Are we doing *things* right?" Using the resources provided as inputs, the library converts them into procedures and processes to provide services (see Figure 5.1). Process measures are concerned about what is done rather than what is achieved and are primarily concerned about cost and time. How much does it cost to perform a task? Which is the best alternative among several options? How do our costs compare to comparable libraries? How much time does it take to perform a task?

A majority of process measures will include cost or time and activity components, for example, the cost of ordering per title, the cost of processing per title, or the elapsed time to receive and process an item. Process measures are designed to help a library improve operations and to demonstrate the responsible use of public funds. These types of measures allow local performance to be placed in a qualitative context, to be compared to the performance of others. Use of staff workload productivity measures on a consistent basis can assist the public library in improving service quality and the efficiency of its operations.[6]

Despite the value and utility of process measures, nothing is less productive than improving the efficiency of what should not be done at all. Lists of process measures that may be of interest to a library are shown in Appendix A. Process measures can be placed in three categories:

- **Efficiency**. Efficiency-related process measures inspect the issue of "how economical is this particular activity?" What is the cost per transaction to provide reference services, document delivery, and any other specific service? How economical is a specific service area such as circulation or technical services?

- **Staff productivity**. Productivity-related measures focus on the time it takes to complete a task or activity. The time for cataloging, time for physical processing, time to receive a journal, and so forth illustrate productivity-related process measures.

- **Library information system activity**. Automated system process measures typically focus on system reliability measures for the computer system itself and for the network, for example, network, server or system availability as expressed as a percent of uptime (99.9 percent) and system reliability as expressed as a percent of downtime (1.1 percent).

Benchmarking

Benchmarking is an organized process for measuring products, services, and practices against external partners to achieve improved performance. Benchmarking is typically associated with the phrase "best practices." There are two forms of benchmarking:

- **Data benchmarking.** This approach measures and compares data about a library's inputs, processes, and outputs to assess performance. Usually data about costs, quality, timeliness, and customer satisfaction for the local library will be compared to comparable libraries within the state and perhaps nationally. The availability of such data allows a library to track its progress toward meeting goals that it has set for itself. The vast majority of benchmarking that is done in libraries and local government is data benchmarking.[7] Although data benchmarking is particularly useful in identifying potential problems or performance gaps compared to other organizations, this approach does not help identify the causes of the differences in performance or indicate how to improve performance.

- **Process benchmarking.** This methodology is concerned with analyzing and understanding a sequence of activities and comparing them to other similar activities in other organizations. A process is a set of linked activities that take an input and transform it to create an output. After learning how well your library does a process now, you discover from others how they do it, and then you apply what has been learned to make your library's operations or service better.

Given that benchmarking, in particular process benchmarking, will require considerable time and resources to complete, any benchmarking project should be for an important process or service (important as defined by the clients of the library or that will have a noteworthy impact on the library's budget or service performance). Not surprisingly, the value of benchmarking is directly related to the effort expended on a benchmarking project, as shown in Figure 5.4. Very few public libraries have been a part of process benchmarking projects.

Benchmarking studies normally select external partners that are within the same industry as well as an external partner known for its excellence in a specific area or process, for example, customer service. This provides a greater range of experiences and assists the library in achieving productivity improvements that are greater than, for example, only selecting peers from within the same industry.[8] The goal is to identify any possible breakthrough innovations, but the results normally are incremental improvements to existing procedures.

Benchmarking normally involves a five-step process,[9] as shown in Figure 5.5.

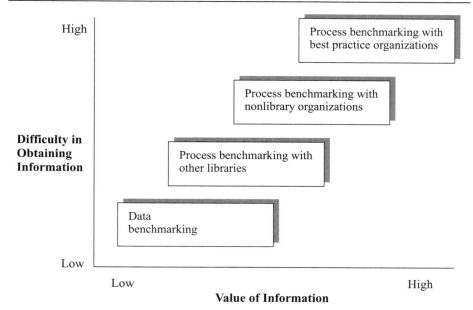

Figure 5.4. Value of Approaches to Benchmarking

1. **Conduct a preliminary analysis**. The needs of three groups should be addressed: public library stakeholders (What are the expectations of library boards, city councils, or county boards of supervisors?), library clients (What functions or services do they deem important?), and library staff members (What service or process do staff feel should be enhanced?).

2. **Develop process measures**. After pinpointing the benchmark focus, the library should first document what it currently does and how well it is doing it. The library might employ such tools as a work process chart (which lists all of the activities, and who performs them, needed to complete the process), an activity flow chart, and/or a fishbone diagram. An important part of this stage of benchmarking is to identify what are the value-added activities as opposed to the nonvalue activities within the library. Nonvalue-adding activities include responding to complaints, correction of errors, redundant files, and duplication of effort. The library should then identify three to seven performance measures it would like to use to judge the same process in the partner organizations.

Figure 5.5. Benchmarking Activities

3. **Identify partners**. Partners will include public libraries, and other types of libraries should also be considered (check with your peers on whom they think are excellent libraries). Nonlibrary partners might include bookstores, video stores, museums, information brokers, as well as mail order and retail stores. G. Arno Loessner developed a practical approach to identify potential benchmarking library partners.[10] Among the selection criteria that needed to be met or exceeded were per capita library budget, per capita acquisitions budget, total staffing, and number of MLS librarians.

4. **Collect and analyze data**. Site visits will be appropriate if the major focus of the benchmarking study is to better understand the process used in the partner organizations (this adds considerably to the time and cost of such a project). Otherwise, the data for each performance measure previously identified are exchanged with the partners.

5. **Present results to management**. A written report describing the results of the benchmarking study is then prepared.

There are a number of benefits associated with the use of benchmarking as an improvement tool:

- improved staff productivity;
- increased understanding of work flows, processes, and procedures;
- new ideas that lead to continuous improvement;
- pride in performance;
- developing a view of service from the user's perspective;
- elimination of barriers between departments and between management and staff;
- reduction in turnaround times;
- reduced error rates; and
- lower operating costs.

All public libraries in England are required to consider the use of benchmarking and outsourcing (and thus the need to better understand the costs associated with each activity) as a part of a mandated program called Best Value.[11] This program mandates that each public library define the values for money and quality of service delivery. The recommended process involves four steps:

- Challenge—is each service really needed?
- Compare—involves analysis, comparison, and benchmarking.

- Consult—involve the customers in a discussion of their needs and preferences.

- Compete—look for private sector involvement and partnerships.

The use of benchmarking can be particularly effective in building a case with the library's funding decision makers to demonstrate how a particular library "stacks up" against other comparable libraries. Showing the same measures over time allows the stakeholders to understand the trends that are occurring in the library. Working with the funding decision makers to set goals, for example, being in the top quartile among the comparable libraries, will be beneficial for the library as it seeks to increase the resources that are allocated to it. This allows the library to state that the goal is become "at least as good as the ABC Public Library."

Output Measures

No measure of performance has any value unless it can be used in some way to influence and improve the process of management.—A. Jones[12]

The use of the library is reflected in output measures. Customers avail themselves of the services offered by the public library and the output measures reflect this usage (see Figure 5.1). These descriptive measures reflect how frequently the library or a specific service is used. Implicit in the use of output measures, especially when utilization is increasing, is that the beneficial effects are also increasing. Among the questions addressed by output measures are: How frequently was the service used? How well was the service provided? How accurate was the information supplied? How approachable was the library staff member? How courteous was the library employee? How satisfied was the client?

The number of books issued is the library world's equivalent of GDP (Gross Domestic Product), the king indicator of economic performance . . .
—Francois Matarasso[13]

Output measures are, in a sense, "feel good" measures since they express how much the library is being used. However, usage is not synonymous with the value or benefits of the library. Output measures can reflect a wide variety of library services and activities, as shown in Appendix A. Output measures can be placed in five general categories:

- **Services**. Output measures generally rely on counts and use per capita statistics. Annual circulation statistics, number of reference questions answered, and attendance at programs are all examples of service-oriented output measures.

- **Quality**. Quality-based output measures ask customers for an appraisal of their satisfaction with a specific library service or of the library in general. Quality does have two important components: *what* is provided to the customer and *how* the service is delivered (the interactions between staff and the customer). Historically, libraries have focused evaluation efforts on "the what" and ignored examining "the how." The use of unobtrusive methods to assess the "correctness and completeness" of reference services is another way to measure the quality of the service being provided.

  George Kroon has suggested that there are four dimensions of quality that should be recognized:[14]

  - *Conformance quality* focuses on reducing errors, defects, or mistakes to improve quality. The tools used to make improvements in this area come from quality engineering, statistical process control, and total quality management.

  - *Quality as expectations* is determined by how well customer expectations are met by actual performance. Customer expectations are influenced by the customer's prior experience, word-of-mouth comments from others, and competitor offerings.

  - *Market perceived quality* compares how well you are doing with respect to your competitors. Benchmarking measurements can be used to assess relative position.

  - *Strategic quality* is the combination of price and quality the organization wants to provide to the market. The quality/price strategy (premium, average, or discount) determines how extensive a service/product offering is, how it is delivered, and so forth.

  The strengths and limitations of each definition are shown in Table 5.1.

- **Collection use**. Collection-oriented output measures are useful for two reasons. First, the degree to which the library's collection is being used is identified. Second, these measures can assist in estimating how well the collection is meeting the needs of the clients. For example, if the turnover rate of a library's collection (annual circulation plus in-house use of materials divided by the total number of volumes) is low, then perhaps the collection is aging or the acquisitions budget has been heavily reduced for the last few years.

Table 5.1. Strengths and Weaknesses of Quality Definitions

Definition	Strengths	Weaknesses
Excellence	Strong marketing benefits Mark of uncompromising standards and high achievement	Provides little practical guidance Measurement difficulties Attributes of excellence may change over time Are customers willing to pay for excellence?
Value	Concept of values incorporates multiple attributes Focuses attention on internal efficiency and external effectiveness Allows for comparisons across objects and experiences	Difficulty extracting individual components of value judgment Questionable inclusiveness of attributes Quality and value are different constructs
Conformance to Specifications	Facilitates precise measurement Leads to increased efficiency Should force disaggregation of customer needs Most appropriate definition for some customers	Most customers do not care about internal specifications Inappropriate measure for services Potentially reduces organizational adaptability Specifications may become obsolete in rapidly changing markets Internally focused
Meeting and/or Exceeding Expectations	Evaluation from customer perspective Applicable across industries Responsive to market changes All-encompassing definition	Most complex definition Difficult to measure Customers may be unaware of their expectations Idiosyncratic reactions Pre-use attitudes affect subsequent judgments Short-term and long-term evaluations may differ Confusion between customer service and customer satisfaction

Adapted from Carol A. Reeves and David A. Bednar. Defining Quality: Alternatives and Implications. *Academy of Management Review,* 19 (3), 1994, 437.

Circulation per capita, a widely used measure of library activity or performance, may actually be an indirect measure of the proportion of a community's population that uses a library and thus should be used with care.[15] And other research has shown that the population of any community that uses a library is affected primarily by the demographic characteristics of the community, over which the library has little control.[16]

The in-library collection and the electronic full-text resources must be evaluated in tandem. More and more the public library's catalog reflects the resources housed in the library as well as links to resources that may be found on the Internet. In addition, a great many library catalogs also provide access to licensed citation/abstract and full-text databases.

- **Library catalog/portal use**. The library catalog, sometimes called the library online catalog or OPAC, is the search engine that supports the library's clients in finding materials of potential value. A variety of measures can be gathered to determine the degree to which the chief finding aid for the library's collection is being successfully used.

- **Building activity**. A public library often has a number of other building or space-related services. These might include meeting rooms, tables and chairs to perform research or reading, photocopiers, and the opportunity to browse the collection looking for something that might stimulate thinking to solve a problem.

Output measures reflect an inward orientation in that they measure how much the library is used. However, there is no clear innate or implied value in activity per se without context. For example, knowing that a library has an annual circulation of one million does not convey much meaning without knowing more about the community and the circulation statistics of libraries of similar size.

Yet, in a somewhat cynical view of the potential use of output measures, Thomas Ballard has suggested that the majority of results of user studies show that the socioeconomic background of the community surrounding the library determines the amount of use and that these results do not vary much from place to place, so there is little that a library manager can do to encourage more use of the public library.[17] Despite this view, there is ample evidence of public libraries having the same demographic characteristics and having quite varied outputs.

A set of performance measures developed for public libraries in Europe is provided in Appendix B. Seventeen quality-oriented performance measures that were selected as a part of an International Federation of Libraries Association (IFLA) project are listed in Appendix C. A set of recommended key performance indicators that focus on eight objectives were developed for the public libraries of the state of Victoria, Australia, as shown in Appendix D.

John Knightly examined the annual reports from 62 public, academic, special, and school libraries and found that 60 percent of the libraries reported quantifiable measures—process and output measures; 21 percent relied on expert opinion—almost all process measures; 14 percent identified costs—all input measures; but *no* library identified the outcomes or actual benefits from using the library.[18] The end result is that almost all libraries reported using very few measures, with the consequence that these measures will likely lead to misleading feedback about the actual performance of the library.

Attempts to use the Public Library Association's recommended output measures (shown in Table 5.2) in a multibranch public library as fundamental indicators of success in reaching selected objectives appeared fruitless when projected increases (of output measures) fell within the margin of error for the library's sample size.[19] It was noted, however, that the process of analyzing and understanding the relationships among and between the measures was more useful than the statistics themselves. That is, an analysis indicated the need to order more duplicate copies to meet user demand.

Table 5.2. Output Measures

Circulation per Capita	In-Library Materials Use per Capita
Library Visits per Capita	Program Attendance per Capita
Reference Transactions per Capita	Reference Fill Rate
Title Fill Rate	Borrower's Fill Rate
Registration as a Percent of Population	Turnover Rate (circulation per volume)
Document Delivery (percent of requests filled within 7 days; 30 days)	

Attempting to understand what the performance measures are indicating with their numerical value, rather than focusing on the number itself, is crucial to the concept of using measures and indicators to deliver better library services. The measures in and of themselves have little value. Their use and interpretation is where the value of performance measures arises. For example, circulation per capita does nothing to explain the value of the collection to the various segments of the community. Comparing the number of reference questions per capita to another library (or group of libraries) does little in explaining why one group of users asked more reference questions than another group. And, of course, the reference question fill rate measure does not provide any indication of the accuracy or value of the answers provided.[20] Ellen Altman and Allan Pratt compared inputs with outputs in 24 U.S. library systems serving cities over 1 million in population with per capita expenditures ranging from $8.33 to $33.17. The output measures included circulation per capita, reference transactions, number of registered borrowers, collection turnover rates, and collection size. Their analysis determined that none of the 24 library systems was in the top quartile for all five output measures and that there was, in fact, no correlation between inputs and outputs or between expenditures and performance.[21] This lack of causality would appear to make it more difficult to suggest a correlation between output measures and library effectiveness.

One of the more frequently employed performance measures is a client satisfaction survey.

Satisfaction

> *Many librarians maintain that only they, the professionals, have the expertise to assess the quality of library service. . . . Such opinions about service, in fact, are irrelevant. The only thing that matters is the customers' opinions, because without users there is no need for libraries except as warehouses.*—Ellen Altman and Peter Hernon[22]

George D'Elia and Sandra Walsh suggested that user satisfaction surveys are useful for evaluating the performance of a library but should not be used to compare presumed levels of performance for libraries serving different communities.[23] In some cases, user satisfaction surveys are used as an indirect assessment of outcomes.

Satisfaction surveys ask the client to assess the quality and utility of library services. If applied in an appropriate manner, a customer satisfaction survey allows the library to learn what matters to customers and apply that information to improve service delivery. Most satisfaction surveys ask the client to evaluate the effectiveness of the service(s) provided and assess the degree to which the client's needs were met. Customer satisfaction, by its very nature, is inward and backward looking (a lagging indicator of performance).[24] The gaps that exist between a customer's expectations and the service actually provided must be reduced over time.

Too often, customer satisfaction is approached as a report card rather than as a source of information about services where improvement and further analysis and thinking are required. Should a library deliver a service that is below what is expected by the customer, then the only result is dissatisfaction. Excitement or delight will only produce very satisfied customers, since the level of service provided is totally unexpected.

Using customer satisfaction data is complicated by the lack of clarity about what customer satisfaction ratings actually measure. A customer's experience with a library service(s) is dictated by a simple formula:

Customer satisfaction = Performance minus expectations.[25]

Customers are pleased when the perceptions of performance meet or exceed customer expectations, as shown in Figure 5.6. Libraries must pay attention to both performance and customer expectations.

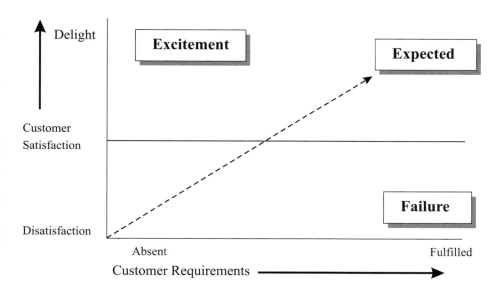

Figure 5.6. Levels of Customer Satisfaction

Satisfaction surveys can be created and conducted by library staff or an outside consultant. If an outside consultant is used, the results of the survey may be better since an organization with experience in designing and administering an "objective" survey will likely produce better results. Further, the stakeholders of the library may be more willing to act upon the recommendations.

There are difficulties associated with a satisfaction survey. These difficulties are usually technical, such as ensuring that an appropriate sample size is obtained, that the sample is random, and that the questions are appropriate worded. However, the chief underlying difficulty connected with any survey is making sure that the right questions are being asked.

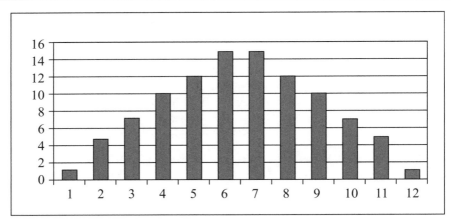

Figure 5.7. Normal Distribution

In any survey, the distribution of satisfaction ratings is presumed to be a reflection of "true" satisfaction. Yet in most customer satisfaction surveys the distribution of responses is abnormally skewed, that is, the majority of the survey respondents report high levels of satisfaction[26] (see Figures 5.7 and 5.8). When considering the results of a satisfaction survey, public libraries must recognize that they are considered a "good thing"—much like apple pie and motherhood.[27] Companies have learned that only when customers rate their buying experience as either completely or extremely satisfied can they count on the customer's repeat purchasing behavior.[28] Perhaps frequent library users are those who rate their library experience as "completely or extremely satisfied."

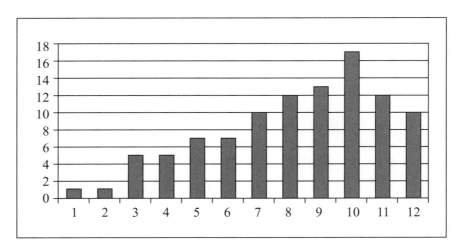

Figure 5.8. Satisfaction Distribution

George D'Elia and Sandra Walsh questioned the value of user satisfaction because users' expectations of a service are conditioned by what they have been used to receiving.[29] In addition, one of the problems with satisfaction surveys is that an individual's expectations may change. An individual may be pleased with a particular product or service (and would rate such a product or service quite high in a satisfaction survey) until he or she discovers an alternative product or service that provides vastly improved levels of satisfaction. Suddenly satisfaction with the old product or service is quite low.[30]

Avoiding Self-Absorption

The typical customer satisfaction survey asks, "How are we doing?" To the extent that this perspective fosters an attitude that the library is well, the library is missing an opportunity to better understand the real needs of its users. As we have seen, the broad customer satisfaction survey responses will typically be very high for the library. But what about the user satisfaction with particular services and products offered by the library? This requires a probing and inquisitive nature and the ability to move beyond the good feelings that arise when the library is rated highly.

Missed Opportunities

Asking users about how *they* are doing, perhaps in a series of focus groups, will reveal the motivations and frustrations that they experience in using the local public library. Perhaps there are real barriers to access and service that can be eliminated that the library is unaware of or never considered from the perspective of the user.

One survey of library users noted that the satisfaction levels were quite high (96 percent) when people succeeded in finding what they wanted but dropped almost in half when they failed to find what they wanted.[31] D'Elia, attempting to ascertain the determinants of user satisfaction in a public library setting, found that there were none. He examined user demographics, the various uses of the library by the user, and the user's evaluation of the characteristics of the library used.[32] Although satisfaction is important as a perceived value of library service, it does not demonstrate how the individual or the community has benefited from the services provided by the public library.

Failing to Understand Expectations

Most often customer satisfaction surveys focus on customer *perceptions* of service delivery but rarely afford the customer an opportunity to articulate *expectations* of service delivery. Since customers compare their expectations with their experiences, having a good understanding of expectations is important to better serve the needs of public library users.

Another problem with satisfaction surveys is that they often fail to probe beneath the surface of responses provided and in fact may be reluctant to criticize libraries generally. However, one study found that people were willing to suggest or agree with specific criticisms or complaints.[33]

Providing a level of service that users rate as satisfactory may not be enough. In fact, different satisfaction levels may reflect different issues and therefore require different corrective actions. Several research studies have demonstrated that only completely satisfied customers will be loyal.[34]

Perspective

In some cases, it is possible to improve the quality, timeliness, and utility of an information service and see a corresponding increase in customer satisfaction surveys over time. Yet even in the face of objective measures that demonstrate improvements in service levels, citizen satisfaction surveys (a subjective measure) might report the same or only slight increases in customer satisfaction levels. This may be the case since input, process, and output measures typically are collected and reported as administrative performance measures, whereas citizens' evaluations are likely to be based on outcomes that are meaningful to them.[35]

Methodology Problems

Satisfaction data collected using different means (in-person or telephone surveys versus self-administered survey forms) are not comparable. In some cases, oral data gathering techniques may increase satisfaction ratings by 10 to 12 percent compared to data gathered using self-administered surveys.[36] Further, how a question is asked appears to affect the level of satisfaction. A positive form of the question ("How satisfied are you?") seems to lead to greater reported levels of satisfaction than a negative form ("How dissatisfied are you?").

Priority Setting

Asking users about the relevance of existing and possible public library services is one form of a client satisfaction survey that can have direct and positive impact. The users will benefit since the library will better appreciate what services have the greatest clear-cut impact on their personal or professional lives. The library, in turn, can benefit from such a survey in that it will identify what services are most important but also understand how the users rate the library's current performance for each specific service offering.

Using a priority and performance evaluation or PAPE survey, the user is asked to indicate the priority the library should give to each service using a Likert scale.[37] Following this, the user is asked to rate the library's performance in providing the service (see a sample PAPE survey instrument in Figure 5.9). In addition to asking users to participate in a PAPE survey, asking the library's funding decision makers and library staff to also complete the questionnaire will allow the library to compare and contrast the responses from these three important groups. Any differences that emerge among the three groups will require further attention and consideration. One PAPE study found that while there was general congruence between library staff and their customers, there was a tendency for library staff members to underestimate the importance of performing the promised service dependably and accurately.[38]

In your opinion, what priority should the library give each of the following?
Please circle the number that best gives an indication of your assessment.

	Low Priority				Very High Priority			Don't Know
	< - >							
Availability and accessibility of								
library staff	1	2	3	4	5	6	7	D
Availability of reference services	1	2	3	4	5	6	7	D
Checking out books	1	2	3	4	5	6	7	D
Able to browse magazines								
and newspapers	1	2	3	4	5	6	7	D
Interlibrary loan service	1	2	3	4	5	6	7	D
Access to online databases	1	2	3	4	5	6	7	D
And so forth . . .								

In your opinion, how well does the library perform in each of the following areas?
Please circle the number that best gives an indication of your assessment.

	Low Priority				Very High Priority			Don't Know
	< - >							
Availability of reference services	1	2	3	4	5	6	7	D
Checking out books	1	2	3	4	5	6	7	D
Availability and accessibility of								
library staff	1	2	3	4	5	6	7	D
Access to online databases	1	2	3	4	5	6	7	D
Interlibrary loan service	1	2	3	4	5	6	7	D
Able to browse magazines								
and newspapers	1	2	3	4	5	6	7	D
And so forth . . .								

Note: The order of the library services in the second question should be different than the sequence of the first question. This forces the respondent to carefully read and rate each library service.

Figure 5.9. Sample PAPE Questionnaire

A sample of the results from a PAPE survey is shown in Figure 5.10. In all, 21 library services have been prioritized and evaluated (identified using the letters of the alphabet). Notice that for the first 14 services, the priority assigned by the library's clients exceeded the library's ability to deliver the expected level of service (with three exceptions). For the services with lower priorities, actual performance exceeded expectations in only two cases. Some adjustment of the service levels for these two highly rated services might be advisable.

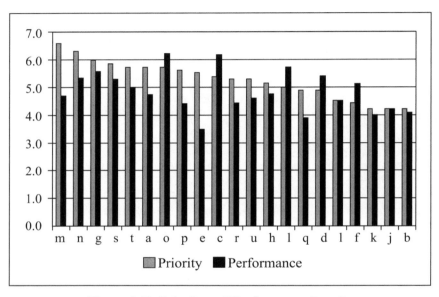

Figure 5.10. Priority and Performance Results

An alternative manner of presenting the PAPE survey results is shown in Figure 5.11. A somewhat similar presentation approach is called a quadrant analysis; it is shown in Figure 5.12. Plotting the scores of priority and performance will allow the library to see what services should be focused on to make improvements that will have the greatest impact on the library's customers.[39]

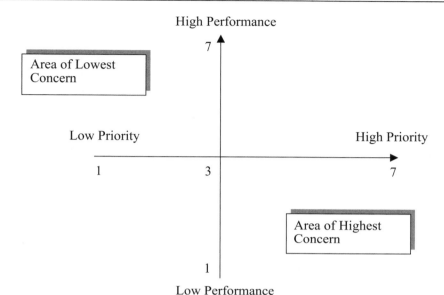

Figure 5.11. User Priority and Performance (Satisfaction) Ratings

Libraries that have used PAPE have found it to be a useful tool that can be administered annually to capture any shifts of the priorities of their users as well as tracking improvements in services provided.

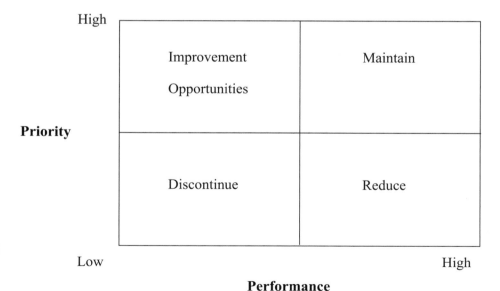

Figure 5.12. Quadrant Analysis Illustration

Service Quality

Service quality has garnered much attention in the professional management and library literature in the last few years. Satisfaction has been defined as "the emotional reaction to a specific transaction or service encounter."[40] Service quality is an antecedent of customer satisfaction, and higher quality service levels will result in increased customer satisfaction. Yet a client can visit the library and obtain a correct answer to a question but be unsatisfied due to a variety of reasons. Some writers have confused or likened service quality with satisfaction.

Satisfaction has two perspectives. The first is *service encounter satisfaction*, which is the degree of satisfaction or dissatisfaction experienced by the individual with a specific service transaction. Jan Carlson, former president of SAS Airlines, coined the phrase "moments of truth" to describe any point in time during which a customer comes into contact with an organization.[41] Examples of "moments of truth" within a public library might include contact at the information desk, reference desk, or circulation desk or asking for assistance from a page in the stacks.

The second component or perspective is *overall service satisfaction*, or the level of client satisfaction or dissatisfaction based on multiple transactions or experiences.[42] The overall service satisfaction is built up over time and is the result of numerous transactions of varying quality. Others have suggested that *customer satisfaction* refers to a specific transaction, whereas *service quality* is the collective judgment based on all of the previous encounters.

A simplified model of the interactions among and between client expectations, perceptions, and satisfaction, their assessment of service quality, and the resulting overall customer satisfaction is shown in Figure 5.13. The various quality-related survey instruments are assessing the "perceived quality" rather than attempting to determine an "objective measure of quality."

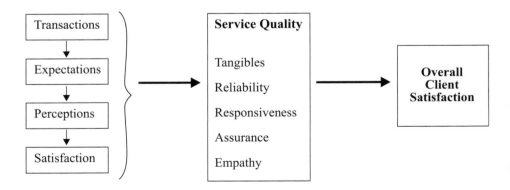

Figure 5.13. Client Satisfaction and Service Quality Model. Adapted from Rowena Cullen. Perspectives on User Satisfaction Surveys. *Library Trends*, 49 (4), Spring 2001, 662–86.

One popular service quality assessment tool, developed in the retail industry and called SERVQUAL (Service Quality), has been adapted for libraries.[43] SERVQUAL compares the expectations of customers and performance using five attributes:

- **Tangibles**. Physical appearance of the library, library staff members, equipment, and communication materials (signage, handouts, and so forth).

- **Reliability**. Is the service reliable and consistent? This is the *most* important factor among the five attributes being evaluated by the client.

- **Responsiveness**. How timely is the service? Are staff members willing to provide assistance?

- **Assurance**. Do staff convey competence and confidence? Are staff knowledgeable, professional, and courteous?

- **Empathy**. Are the staff member cheerful? Do they provide individualized attention to the client?

A shorter, competing survey instrument, called SERVPERF (Service Performance), was developed to better address the issue of predicting overall variance.[44]

It is possible to use the data gathered by SERQUAL to identify five different gaps, as shown in Figure 5.14. The *service quality gap* arises from the difference between the perceived service and the expected service. Other gaps will likely be contributing to the service quality gap.

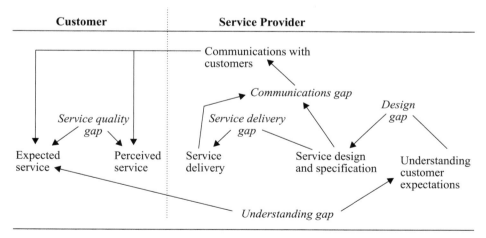

Figure 5.14. Service Quality Gaps. Adapted from Mik Wisniewski and Mike Donnelly. Measuring Service Quality in the Public Sector: The Potential for SERVQUAL. *Total Quality Management,* **7 (4), 1996, 357–65.**

The *understanding gap* comes about due to the differences between customer service expectations and management's understanding of customer expectations. Such a gap may arise due to a less-than-clear understanding of customer needs or poor communication within the library.

The *design gap* is the gap between management's understanding of customer expectations and the design and specifications of service quality. The management team provides the training to the library's employees about what constitutes acceptable levels of service. The *delivery gap* will arise due to the gap between the specification of service quality and the actual quality of service delivered.

Finally, the *communications gap* is between what is actually delivered and what has been promised in terms of external communications, comparison by the customer of experiences with other similar services, and so forth.

There have been several criticisms of the SERVQUAL approach, including fundamental measurement problems, the belief that use of perceptions is better than use of this particular scale, shortcomings in how the scale was developed, use of a scale that includes both positive and negative wording of questions, and the fact that use of the scale across organizations can be problematic.[45] These problems arise, in part, because the data are collected after a service encounter, and questions about service expectations may be based on memory or biased by the services actually received. Version of SERVQUAL have been used in a number of library settings with success.[46]

One adaptation of SERVQUAL, which has been named LibQUAL+, has been pilot tested by a large number of Association of Research Libraries since the spring of 2000. Initially five dimensions were identified as being useful for assessing library service: affect of service, reliability, library as place, provision of physical collections, and access to information.[47] Through the extensive testing of the instrument, LibQUAL+ has been refined and now includes 25 survey questions providing information about four dimensions:[48]

- **Service affect**
  - Empathy
  - Responsiveness
  - Assurance
  - Reliability
- **Library as place**
  - Utilitarian space
  - Symbol
  - Refuge

- **Personal control**
  - Ease of navigation
  - Convenience
  - Modern equipment
- **Information access**
  - Content/scope
  - Timeliness
  - Convenience

When using LibQUAL+ data can be collected from different groups. Thus, clients, stakeholders, and library staff could be surveyed. An analysis of the differences and similarities in the ratings between the groups can be revealing and helpful in assessing the quality of library services. The availability and utility of the LibQUAL+ instrument for use outside of the Association of Research Libraries is yet to be determined. An alternative analysis of customer satisfaction suggests that librarians should focus on the library's resources (its collection and providing access to electronic resources) and staff demeanor or attitude.[49]

An individual can also have valid reasons for dissatisfaction after a visit to the library. For example, the individual might receive a correct negative to an unanswerable question, not receive an answer at the time (but could have done so if more time had been available), or receive an answer not satisfactory to the user even though the answer was correct.[50]

In addition to conducting surveys of customer satisfaction and quality assessment, a library might perform a "walk-through audit" to assess the total customer experience.[51] The audit comprises a number of questions to be answered by a team of library managers that take the managers through the customer's experience stage by stage. The results of the audit can highlight areas the library can change to improve the "experience" of going to the library.

Defining Service Characteristics

One of the challenges facing any service provider, such as a public library, is gaining an understanding of what service characteristics are expected as a matter of course and what characteristics will delight the customer. Dr. Noriaki Kano, a Japanese quality expert, developed the "Kano model" to assist in this process. Kano's model predicts the degree of customer satisfaction, which is dependent upon the degree of fulfillment of customer requirements and that customers have different types of customer expectations.

The Kano model relates three factors to their degree of implementation, as shown in Figure 5.15 (page 100): basic or expected (must be) factors, normal or fundamental (more is better) factors, and delighter or latent (excitement) factors. The degree of customer satisfaction ranges from disgust, through neutrality, to delighted.

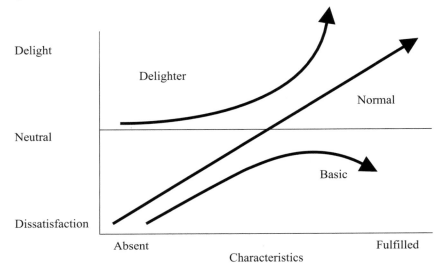

Figure 5.15. The Kano Model

Basic requirements are those that are so obvious to customers that they do not state them overtly. They are normally so obviously essential to the customer that stating these requirements seems a bit silly. For example, you would expect to hear a dial tone when you pick up a telephone. If you don't, then you are unhappy. Failing to provide basic requirements will result in customer complaints.

Normal requirements are those that a customer is cognizant of and can readily articulate. When these needs are met, customers are satisfied and when they are not met, dissatisfaction arises. If more than "standard" customer requirements are delivered, then additional perceived benefits are generated.

Delighter requirements or exciting requirements are needs that some or all customers may not be aware of. These are often referred to as latent requirements. These are "out of the ordinary" services, product features, or characteristics. If a provider understands such a need and fulfills it, the customer is delighted and will respond with a "wow" reaction. If these needs are not met there is no customer response since customers are unaware of the need.

A library can analyze an existing or planned service by involving users to discover the types of customer requirements. This is done by using a two-sided question. The same question is asked of a number of users in positive and negative forms, for example:

- How do you feel if our service has feature X?

- How do you feel if our service does not have feature X?

The respondent is presented with four choices for these two questions:

- I like it.
- It is normally that way (feature is expected).
- I don't care.
- I don't like it.

The results are then tallied. Features or requirements that have high counts represent one of the three types of customer requirements, as shown in Table 5.3. It should be remembered that over time, some service characteristics will move from delightful to normal and from normal to basic.

Table 5.3. Kano Model Response Table

		Negative Question Answers			
		Like	Normal	Don't Care	Don't Like
Positive Question Answers	**Like**		Delightful	Delightful	Normal
	Normal				Basic
	Don't Care				Basic
	Don't Like				

A library can use this methodology to systematically examine all of the characteristics and features of a service to discover what characteristics are particularly important to the user. These service characteristics can be identified by using a systems analysis approach to break a service down into its component steps and processes. This can be complemented by observing users as they interact with the service. Some of the issues that should be addressed are the following:[52]

- What do customers find frustrating and/or confusing about the service?
- Does the user experience any anxiety using the service?
- Are there any time-consuming or wasteful activities involved in using the service?
- What things does the user do that are "wrong"?
- What is causing a customer to use the service once and not return?
- Are there any other irritants that are experienced by a user when using the service?

The library might also use focus groups to identify other characteristics or features of a particular library service, such as circulation and reference.

Summary

Use of input, process, and output measures, including satisfaction and service quality measures, can provide an important perspective on just how well the public library is doing. Tracking the same measures over time allows the library to know if use of its services is declining or increasing.

Given the glut of performance measures that can be collected, the library should carefully assess what measures will be collected so that busy staff are not overwhelmed by the data collection process. More important, the selection of measures is crucial so that library managers can have a clearer picture of the effects of their services on their customers, and funding decision makers will have more confidence that the citizens (and voters) of a community are being well served by their local public library. In short, it is important to demonstrate economy or efficiency in operation as well as providing "value" to the community.

Notes

1. Robert Swisher and Charles R. McClure. *Research for Decision Making: Methods for Librarians*. Chicago: American Library Association, 1984.

2. American Library Association. *Public Library Service: A Guide to Evaluation with Minimum Standards*. Chicago: American Library Association, 1956; L. Carnovsky. Public Library Surveys and Evaluations. *Library Quarterly*, 25, 1955, 23–36; F. B. Murray. Canadian Library Standards. *Library Trends*, 21, 1972, 298–311; Public Library Association, Professional Standards Committee. *Minimum Standards for Public Library Systems*. Chicago: American Library Association, 1967.

3. Walt Crawford. *Technical Standards: An Introduction for Librarians*. 2nd ed. Boston: G. K. Hall, 1991.

4. See chapter 10 of F. W. Lancaster, *The Measurement and Evaluation of Library Services* (Washington, DC: Information Resources Press, 1977) for an extensive review of the history of library standards.

5. David N. Ammons. Overcoming the Inadequacies of Performance Measurement in Local Government: The Case of Libraries and Leisure Services. *Public Administration Review*, 55 (1), 1995, 37–47.

6. Catherine A. Larson. Customers First: Using Processing Improvement to Improve Service Quality and Efficiency. *Reference Services Review*, 26 (1), Spring 1998, 51–60, 96+.

7. David N. Ammons. Raising the Performance Bar . . . Locally. *Public Management*, 79 (9), September 1997, 10–18.

8. Robert C. Camp. *Business Process Benchmarking: The Search for Industry Best Practices That Lead to Superior Performance*. Milwaukee, WI: ASQC Quality Press, 1995.

9. Holly J. Muir. *Conducting a Preliminary Benchmarking Analysis: A Librarian's Guide*. Cincinnati, OH: Library Benchmarking International, 1993; Holly J. Muir. *Developing Benchmarking Metrics: A Librarian's Guide*. Cincinnati, OH: Library Benchmarking International, 1993; Holly J. Muir. *Identifying Benchmarking Partners: Special Libraries*. Cincinnati, OH: Library Benchmarking International, 1993; Holly J. Muir. *Collecting & Analyzing Benchmarking Data: A Librarian's Guide*. Cincinnati, OH: Library Benchmarking International, 1993; Holly J. Muir. *Presenting Benchmarking Results: A Librarian's Guide*. Cincinnati, OH: Library Benchmarking International, 1993.

10. G. Arno Loessner. Estimating Local Financial Support for Public Libraries. *Public Productivity & Management Review*, 23 (1), September 1999, 24–39.

11. Leo Favret. Benchmarking, Annual Library Plans and Best Value: The Implications for Public Libraries. *Library Management*, 21 (7), 2000, 340–48.

12. A. Jones. Existing Output Measures and Their Inadequacies, in *Output Measurement*. London: Public Libraries Research Group, 1974.

13. Francois Matarasso. *Beyond Book Issues: The Social Potential of Library Projects*. London: The British Library and Comedia, 1998, 50.

14. George E. Kroon. Improving Quality in Service Marketing: Four Important Dimensions. *Journal of Customer Service in Marketing & Management*, 1 (2), 1995, 13–28.

15. George D'Elia and Sandra Walsh. Patrons' Uses and Evaluations of Library Services: A Comparison Across Five Public Libraries. *Library and Information Science Review*, 7, 1985, 3–30.

16. George D'Elia. The Development and Testing of a Conceptual Model of Public Library User Behavior. *Library Quarterly*, 50, 1980, 410–30.

17. Ballard, Thomas H. Planning and Output Measures. *Public Libraries*, 28, 1989, 292–94.

18. John J. Knightly. Overcoming the Criterion Problem in the Evaluation of Library Performance. *Special Libraries*, 70, April 1979, 173–79.

19. Laura J. Seff. Management Uses of Output Measures at Branch and Systems Level in Baltimore County Public Library. *Public Libraries*, 26 (3), 1987, 120–22.

20. Teresa Manthey and Jeanne Owen Brown. Evaluating a Special Library Using Public Library Measures. *Special Libraries*, 76 (4), 1985, 282–89.

21. Ellen Altman and Peter Pratt. Live by the Numbers, Die by the Numbers. *Library Journal*, 122, April 15, 1997, 48–49.

22. Ellen Altman and Peter Hernon. Service Quality and Customer Satisfaction Do Matter. *American Libraries*, August 1998, 53–54.

23. George D'Elia and Sandra Walsh. User Satisfaction with Library Service—A Measure of Public Library Performance? *The Library Quarterly*, 53 (2), April 1983, 109–33.

24. Jennifer Cram. Six Impossible Things Before Breakfast: A Multidimensional Approach to Measuring the Value of Libraries. Keynote Address to the Third Northumbria International Conference on Performance Measurement in Libraries and Information Services, August 27–31, 1999. Available at http://www.alia.org.au/~jcram/six_things.html (accessed June 16, 2003).

25. Richard L. Lynch and Kelvin F. Cross. *Measure Up! Yardsticks for Continuous Improvement.* London: Basil Blackwell, 1991.

26. Douglas Badenoch, Christine Reid, Paul Burton, Forbes Gibb, and Charles Oppenheim. The Value of Information, in Mary Feeney and Maureen Grieves (Eds.). *The Value and Impact of Information.* London: Bowker Saur, 1994, 9–78.

27. Ruth Applegate. Models of User Satisfaction: Understanding False Positives. *RQ*, 32 (4), 1993, 525–39.

28. Thomas O. Jones and W. Earl Sasser Jr. Why Satisfied Customers Defect. *Harvard Business Review*, November–December 1995, 88–99.

29. George D'Elia, and Sandra Walsh. User Satisfaction with Library Service—Measure of Public Library Performance? *Library Quarterly*, 53 (2), 1983, 109–33.

30. John Guaspari. The Hidden Costs of Customer Satisfaction. *Quality Digest*, February 1998, 45–49.

31. Totterdell and Bird. *Effective Library.*

32. George D'Elia. User Satisfaction As a Measure of Public Library Performance, in: *Library Effectiveness: A State of the Art. Papers from a 1980 ALA Preconference, June 27 & 28, 1980, New York, NY.* Chicago: American Library Association, 1980, 64–69.

33. Totterdell and Bird. *Effective Library.*

34. Jones and Sasser. Why Satisfied Customers Defect.

35. Janet M. Kelly and David Swindell. A Multiple-Indicator Approach to Municipal Service Evaluation: Correlating Performance Measurement and Citizen Satisfaction Across Jurisdictions. *Public Administration Review*, 62 (5), September/October 2002, 610–21.

36. Robert A. Peterson and William R. Wilson. Measuring Customer Satisfaction: Fact and Artifact. *Journal of the Academy of Marketing Science*, 20 (1), Winter 1992, 61–71.

37. Marianne Broadbent and Hans Lofgren. Information Delivery: Identifying Priorities, Performance and Value. *OPAC and Beyond. Victorian Association for Library Automation 6ᵗʰ Biennial Conference and Exhibition, 11–13 November 1991, Hilton on the Park, Melbourne, Australia*, 185–215; Marianne Broadbent. Demonstrating Information Service Value to Your Organization. *Proceedings of the IOLIM Conference*, 16, 1992, 65–83; Marianne Broadbent and Hans Lofgren. *Priorities, Performance and Benefits: An Exploratory Study of Library and Information Units.* Melbourne, Australia: CIRCIT Ltd. and ACLIS, 1991.

38. Susan Edwards and Mairead Browne. Quality in Information Services: Do Users and Librarians Differ in Their Expectations. *Library & Information Science Review*, 17, 1995, 163–82.

39. Danuta A. Nitecki. Quality Assessment Measures in Libraries. *Advances in Librarianship*, 25, 2001, 133–62.

40. K. Elliott. A Comparison of Alternative Measures of Service Quality. *Journal of Customer Service in Marketing and Management*, I (1), 1995, 35.

41. Jan Carlson. *Moments of Truth.* Cambridge, MA: Balinger, 1987.

42. Peter Hernon and Ellen Altman. *Assessing Service Quality: Satisfying the Expectations of Library Customers.* Chicago: American Library Association, 1998; see also Peter Hernon and Ellen Altman. *Service Quality in Academic Libraries.* Norwood, NJ: Ablex, 1996.

43. A. Parasuraman, Valarie A. Zeithaml, and Leonard L. Berry. SERVQUAL: A Multiple-item Scale for Measuring Consumer Perceptions of Service Quality. *Journal of Retailing*, 64, 1988, 12–37; Valarie A. Zeithaml, A. Parasuraman, and Leonard L. Berry. *Delivering Quality Service: Balancing Customer Perceptions and Expectations.* New York: Free Press, 1990; A. Parasuraman, Valarie A. Zeithaml, and Leonard L. Berry. Reassessment of Expectations As a Comparison Standard in Measuring Service Quality: Implications for Further Research. *Journal of Marketing*, 58 (1), January 1994, 111–24.

44. Joseph J. Cronin and Steven A. Taylor. SERVPERF Versus SERVQUAL: Reconciling Performance-Based and Perceptions Minus Expectations of Service Quality. *Journal of Marketing*, 58 (1), January 1994, 125–31.

45. See, for example, Tom J. Brown, Gilbert A Churchill Jr., and J. Paul Peter. Improving the Measurement of Service Quality. *Journal of Retailing*, 66 (1), Spring 1993, 127–39; J. Joseph Cronin Jr. and Stephen A. Taylor. Measuring Service Quality: A Reexamination and Extension. *Journal of Marketing*, 56 (3), July 1992, 55–68; James M. Carman. Consumer Perceptions of Service Quality: An Assessment of SERVQUAL Dimensions. *Journal of Retailing*,

66 (1), Spring 1990, 33–55; Emin Babakus and Gregory W. Boller. An Empirical Assessment of the SERVQUAL Scale. *Journal of Business Research*, 24 (3), Winter 1994, 253–68; Syed Saad Andaleeb and Amiya K. Basu. Technical Complexity and Consumer Knowledge As Moderators of Service Quality Evaluation in the Automobile Industry. *Journal of Retailing*, 70 (4), Winter 1994, 367–81.

46. Syed S. Andaleeb and Patience L. Simmonds. Explaining User Satisfaction with Academic Libraries. *College and Research Libraries,* 59, March 1998, 156–67; Vicki Coleman, Yi (Daniel) Xiao, Linda Bair, and Bill Chollett. Toward a TQM Paradigm: Using SERVQUAL to Measure Library Service Quality. *College & Research Libraries,* 58, May 1997, 237–51; Susan Edwards and Mairead Browne. Quality in Information Services: Do Users and Librarians Differ in Their Expectations? *Library & Information Science Research,* 17, Spring 1995, 163–82.

47. Colleen Cook, Fred Heath, and Bruce Thompson. LibQUAL+: One Instrument in the New Measures Toolbox. Available at: http://www.arl.org/newsltr/212/libqual.html (accessed June 16, 2003); Colleen Cook and Bruce Thompson. Higher-order Factor Analytic Perspectives on Users' Perceptions of Library Service Quality. *Library Information Science Research*, 22, 2000, 393–404; Colleen Cook and Bruce Thompson. Users' Hierarchical Perspectives on Library Service Quality: A LibQUAL+ Study. *College and Research Libraries*, 62, 2001, 147–53.

48. Yvonna S. Lincoln. Insights into Library Services and Users from Qualitative Research. *Library & Information Science Research*, 24 (1), 2002, 3–16.

49. Syed Saad Andaleeb and Patience L. Simmonds. Explaining User Satisfaction with Academic Libraries: Strategic Implications. *College & Research Libraries*, 59, March 1998, 156–67.

50. Knight, Roy. The Measurement of Reference Use, in *Output Measurement*. London: Public Libraries Research Group, 1974.

51. Jennifer Rowley. Customer Experience of Libraries. *Library Review*, 43 (6), 1994, 7–17.

52. Kurt R. Hofmeister, Christi Walters, and John Gongos. Discovering Customer Wow's. *ASQC 50th Annual Quality Conference Proceedings, May 13–15, 1996.* Milwaukee, WI: ASQC, 1996, 759–70.

Chapter 6

Outcomes or Benefits
of a Public Library

Outcome measurement has the potential to be a powerful tool to help us substantiate the claims we know to be true about the impact of libraries in our institutions and in our society.—Peggy Rudd[1]

As noted in the previous chapter, an output is an end product of a service, in this case a library service, and implies a customer exposure to that service. Broadly speaking, outcomes indicate the effect of this exposure on the customer. It is also important to note that outcomes can be planned (sometimes called goals) or unintended, and that the actual outcomes may be less than, equal to, or greater than what was intended.

Tefko Saracevic and Paul Kantor developed a framework and taxonomy for establishing the value that may arise from using library and information services based on the vocabulary of users in responding to a questionnaire.[2] They suggest that a client has three potential reasons to use a library or information service: (1) to work on a task or project; (2) for personal reasons; or (3) to get an object, information, or perform an activity.

They also state that when a client interacts with a library service, there are three areas of interaction that should be considered:

- **Resources**. From the client's perspective, there are three perspectives that might be considered in this area:

    - *Availability*. This traditional evaluation measure attempts to assess whether the library has the given resource, item, or service desired by the client.

107

- *Accessibility*. This measure focuses on the ease with which the service can be accessed. Is a visit to the library required, for example?

- *Quality*. This measure assesses the degree to which a service or resource is accurate, current, timely, and complete.

• **Use of resources and services**. In examining this area, the library could ask its clients to assess five potential measures:

- The degree of *convenience* in using the resource or service.

- The *ease of use*. How difficult is it to use a resource or library service?

- What *frustration*, if any, results from using the resource or library service?

- How *successful* is the client in using a library service or resource?

- How much *effort* is required to move from one service to another? For example, how much effort does it take to perform a search to identify citations and then retrieve the desired journal articles or other resources.

• **Operations and environment**. There are four categories in which clients can be asked to rate the library and its services:

- How reasonable and clear are the library's *policies and procedures*? Do they facilitate access to the library's services or act as impediments?

- Are the *facilities* of adequate size? Do the physical layout and organization of the library resources facilitate access to the resources and services?

- Are library *staff members* helpful, efficient, and knowledgeable? Is there a clear understanding of the goals and objectives of the organization and a desire by library staff to offer a quality service?

- Is the *equipment* reliable and easy to use? Are user instructions or guides readily available?

But most important, Saracevic and Kantor focused on the results, outcomes, or the impact that a library or information service has directly on the individual and indirectly on the organization. Given a reason to use the library, and having had an interaction with one or more library services, what is the effect? They grouped this impact into five categories:

- **Cognitive results**. Use of the library may have an impact on the mind of the client. The intent of this category is to ask the question, "What was learned?" Thus, the client may have

  - refreshed memory of detail or facts;
  - substantiated or reinforced knowledge or belief;
  - gained new knowledge;
  - changed viewpoint, outlook, or perspective;
  - obtained ideas with a slightly different or tangential perspective (serendipity); or
  - obtained no ideas.

- **Affective results**. Use of the library or its services may influence or have an emotional impact on the client. The client may experience

  - a sense of accomplishment, success, or satisfaction;
  - a sense of confidence, reliability, and trust;
  - a sense of comfort, happiness, and good feelings;
  - a sense of failure; or
  - a sense of frustration.

- **Meeting expectations**. When using the library or an information service, clients may

  - be getting what they needed, sought, or expected;
  - be getting too much;
  - be getting nothing;
  - have confidence in what they have received;
  - receive more than expected; or
  - seek substitute sources or action if what they received did not meet their expectations.

- **Accomplishments** in relation to tasks. As a result of using the library, the client is

  - able to make better-informed decisions;
  - achieving a higher quality performance;
  - able to point to a course of action;
  - proceeding to the next step;
  - discovering people and/or other sources of information; or
  - improving a policy, procedure, and plan.

- **Time aspects**. Some of the real value of a library for the client is the fact that the information provided might lead to the saving of time in several possible ways. The client may

    - save time as a result of using the service,

    - waste time as a result of using the service,

    - have to wait for service,

    - experience a service that ranges from slow to fast, or

    - need time to understand how to use a service or resource.

- **Money aspects**. Using the library or information service may, in some cases, clearly result in saving money or generating new revenues. The client may be able to provide an estimate of

    - the dollar value of results obtained from a service or information received,

    - the amount of money saved due to the use of the service,

    - the cost in using the service,

    - what may be spent on a substitute service, or

    - value (in dollars) lost when the service was not available or use was not successful.

Saracevic and Kantor used a survey instrument as well as recording the comments and observations of users to assess the outcome or impact of the library and its information services on the clients of the library. Unfortunately, the model developed by Saracevic and Kantor, while comprehensive, is long and difficult to replicate. It should be noted that the first three results (cognitive, affective, and expectations) would normally translate in some way to having an impact on the latter three outcomes (accomplishments, time, and money). In addition, if there is no link between a cognitive aspect, for example, refreshing an individual's memory about a fact, and a time or money outcome, then that particular information transaction is not directly affecting the organization and would not be "counted" as a measurable outcome.

When collecting evidence about the value of the library to the community and its impact on people's lives, there are four primary roles that can be examined and reported:

- *Traditional functions*—reading and literacy, providing access to information and leisure reading, and education;

- *Social and caring roles*—including personal development, community empowerment and learning, local image, and social cohesion;

- *Equity* between groups and communities as well as equity of access; and

- *Economic impact*—including business and employment information, training opportunities, and tourism information.

The various approaches to identifying the value of a public library are summarized in Figure 6.1. These approaches can be divided into two broad groups: economic and social.

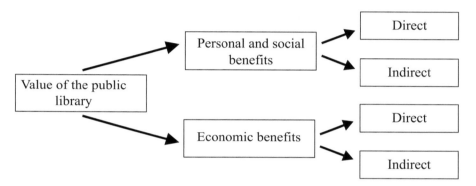

Figure 6.1. Categories of Possible Public Library Benefits

There is also a tradition of not evaluating services provided by public-sector organizations for a variety of reasons. Fewer than 40 percent of municipal jurisdictions make any kind of meaningful use of performance measures in their management and decision processes. This despite the fact that, when performance measures are actively embraced, service quality is improved, there is increased accountability of managers, and employees are more likely to focus on organizational goals.[3] However, as David Osborne and Ted Gaebler note, there are a number of consequences associated with a laissez faire approach to performance measurement:[4]

- What gets measured gets done.

- If results aren't measured, it is difficult to tell success from failure.

- If success can't be seen, it is difficult to reward it.

- If success is not rewarded, failure is either being ignored or rewarded.

- If success can't be seen, it is difficult to learn from it.

- If failure is not recognized, it can't be corrected.

- If results cannot be demonstrated, it is difficult to gain public support.

Of course, the problem of attempting to assess outcomes is complicated by the fact that the benefits from the use of the public library may accrue directly to the individual user, indirectly to the community, or both. In addition to the traditional use of input, process, and output measures, some researchers and public libraries have attempted to identify either the social benefits or economic benefits that occur as the result of using the local library. Yet, as will be seen in the next two chapters, there are problems associated with the measurement of these benefits.

One very readable report—*Dividends: The Value of Public Libraries in Canada*—identified the many economic and social impacts of public libraries on Canadian society.[5] Yet even after a careful review of this document, the reader is somewhat confused by the plethora of approaches that can be used to assert the value of the public library. The issue remains: How do we choose?

A part of the answer lies in what the focus of the performance measures being used by the public library is? As shown in Figure 6.2, performance measures can have an internal or an external focus.

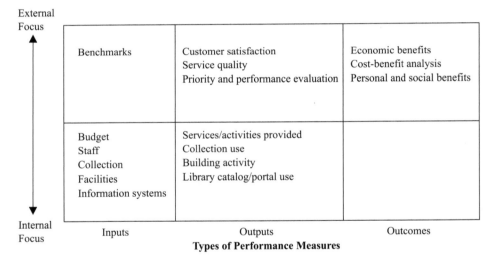

Figure 6.2. A Focus Measurement Matrix

Summary

This chapter has demonstrated that there are a variety of ways to attempt to determine the value of a library and the services that it provides. A public library is going to have great difficulty in assessing the value of the library for individual users, businesses, and the community itself. Yet there are approaches available to assist the library in identifying the possible social and economic benefits of the public library.

Notes

1. *Perspectives on Outcomes Based Evaluation for Libraries and Museums.* Washington, DC: Institute of Museums and Library Services, 2000.

2. Tefko Saracevic and Paul B. Kantor. Studying the Value of Library and Information Services. Part I. Establishing a Theoretical Framework. *Journal of the American Society of Information Science*, 48 (6), 1997, 527–42; Tefko Saracevic and Paul B. Kantor. Studying the Value of Library and Information Services. Part II. Methodology and Taxonomy. *Journal of the American Society of Information Science*, 48 (6), 1997, 543–63.

3. Theodore H. Poister and Gregory Streib. Performance Measurement in Municipal Government: Assessing the State of the Practice. *Public Administration Review*, 59 (4), July/August 1999, 325–35.

4. David Osborne and Ted Gaebler. *Reinventing Government: How the Entrepreneurial Spirit Is Transforming the Public Sector.* New York: Addison-Wesley, 1992.

5. Leslie Fitch and Jody Warner. Dividends: The Value of Public Libraries in Canada. *The Bottom Line*, 11 (4), 1998, 158–79.

Chapter

Social Benefits

7

The social benefits that arise from the range of services provided by public libraries are generally well known and recognized by both librarians and the citizens within a community. The positive contributions of a public library are many and some of the frequently cited social benefits maybe found in Figure 7.1 (page 116). Public libraries are meritorious since they maintain or improve literacy, stimulate the imagination, and expand personal horizons. Because the local library provides access to a variety of information resources, it informs and empowers citizens in a democratic society. And yet, as an intangible asset within a community, a great deal of the public library's value lies in the future.

By its fundamental nature, a public library provides access to information and the library's services to anyone. The wide range of information services that are available under one roof contributes to the strength and appeal of the library. The benefit for the individual user is convenience.

It is possible to consider the social benefits or impacts of the public library as the meaning of the library to the community it serves. These benefits can be divided into two groups depending on their impact on the individual and on the community, as noted in Table 7.1 (page 117). It is also conceivable to view the public library as an institution that accumulates social capital as a byproduct of its interactions; this view results in a sense that the library enhances the functioning of the wider society.

❑ Public libraries support preschool, elementary, and high school education through a variety of complementary services and providing access to resources.

❑ Public libraries support self-directed education and skill development.

❑ Public libraries provide literacy services from preschool to adult age individuals.

❑ Public libraries support job-seekers by offering information and pertinent resources.

❑ Public libraries work with employment services.

❑ Public libraries support small businesses and self-employed people.

❑ Public libraries provide access to computers and the Internet.

❑ Public libraries present basic information technology training.

❑ Public libraries provide out-of-school activities for young people.

❑ Public libraries offer meeting places and educational resources for children.

❑ Public libraries provide access to information about private and public social services.

❑ Public libraries are often used by people with low incomes

❑ Public libraries provide access to health information and services.

❑ Public libraries contribute to the quality of life through leisure opportunities.

❑ Public libraries provide services appealing to older people.

❑ Public libraries assist in community development.

❑ Public libraries provide services to isolated people.

❑ Public libraries offer outreach services to minority populations.

❑ Public libraries provide a sense of place within a community.

❑ Public libraries facilitate people's involvement in local, state, and national democracy.

Figure 7.1. The Social Impact of Public Libraries

Table 7.1. Social Benefits

Individual	Community
Use of leisure time	Social interactions
Informed personal decisions	Community awareness
Literacy	Literacy
Support of education —for children —for teenagers —for adults	Support for a democratic society
Lifelong learning	
Local history and genealogy	

Summarizing the results of a number of studies that attempted to identify the social impact of the public library, Barbara Debono found that three or more of these studies articulated the following social impacts:[1]

- increased quality of life,
- access to culture and the arts,
- equity/free access to resources,
- improved personal development,
- vocational and/or economic effects,
- recreation,
- community building,
- decreasing social isolation,
- education,
- health and general information, and
- public space.

Use of Leisure Time

The raison d'être for a large number of public library users is the ability to borrow materials for leisure time use. For a majority of these library users, that means being able to check out popular fiction and nonfiction books or fiction within a particular genre or by a favorite author. The ability to borrow videos and

DVDs, audiotapes and CDs (books on tape and learning materials as well as music) is one that is appreciated and valued by these citizens.

Yet the library clearly faces a significant amount of competition in that people make choices to engage in other leisure time activities, as shown in Figure 7.2. Reading is fifth in popularity after television, listening to music, reading the newspaper and magazines, and logging on to the Internet. Demonstrating that the library serves a large portion of the community's leisure time activities on a regular basis is an important message to convey to the library's stakeholders.

A research project called the Counting on Results Project was designed to develop service-specific outcome measures, and it collected information from several thousand patrons. Each of the libraries participating in the study was allowed to select one or more service responses and then would distribute a short survey to its patrons that focused on that specific service response (with the result that the size of the sample for each service response varies). The Counting on Results Project found that "general information" applies to the greatest number of library users. In addition, it should not be surprising that 74 percent of the Counting on Results Project general information respondents indicated that leisure reading was the dominant outcome.[2] A summary of the general nformation outcomes is provided in Table 7.2 (page 120).

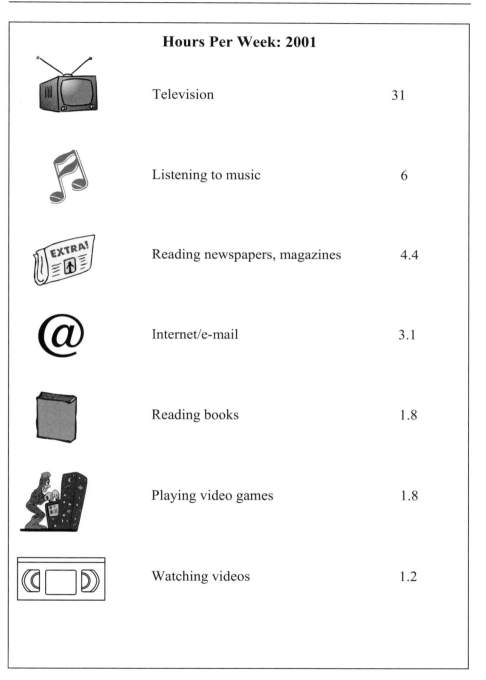

Hours Per Week: 2001

Television	31
Listening to music	6
Reading newspapers, magazines	4.4
Internet/e-mail	3.1
Reading books	1.8
Playing video games	1.8
Watching videos	1.2

Figure 7.2. Leisure Time Activities. Adapted from Table 1125: Media Usage and Consumer Spending, in *Statistical Abstract of the United States: 2001. The National Data Book*. Washington, DC: U.S. Government Printing Office, 2001.

Table 7.2. General Information Outcomes

Outcomes	Percent Selected
Read for pleasure	74
Learned more about a skill, hobby, or other personal interest	56
Found information for school, work, or a community group	46
Obtained a specific fact or document	42
Learned more about a legal, social, or political issue	24

Readers choose books for the pleasure anticipated in the reading itself and sometimes, serendipitously, they encounter material that helps them in the context of their lives.[3] And while readers find nonfiction works valuable for obtaining specific information on a known topic, they also find works of fiction to have value.

Potential performance measures to demonstrate the use of the library for leisure time activities include proportion of the community that is library users, demographic profile of the library users, circulation of recreational reading materials per capita, participation in book clubs, and circulation of audiovisual materials per capita.

Assessment: Good. The public library is able to present an accurate picture of how the library's resources are being used by the community for leisure time activities.

Informed Personal Decisions

The library's collection contains a wide range of materials about raising a family, jobs, hobbies, history, science, drugs, health, travel, and so forth. These materials can help individuals learn more about themselves, their families, working with others, their community, and their country. In short, there is a surplus of materials to assist individuals in making more informed decisions about a variety to issues that will arise as they go through life.

A public library also typically provides reference services to assist individuals in finding the materials they are seeking.

Assessment: Poor. It is very difficult to develop a set of performance measures that would somehow indicate use of these materials and how they enrich the lives of individuals.

Literacy

Some libraries provide a literacy program, typically using volunteers as tutors, to assist individuals in improving their reading skills. Typically libraries employ a variety of techniques, including individual tutoring, computer-assisted instruction and skills assessment, and small group discussions as a means to improve literacy in an individual. In some cases, the literacy program will also provide English as a Second Language (ESL) classes. For some individuals, the literacy program means that they can improve their reading skills so that they can prepare for and pass the Graduation Equivalent Degree (GED) examination. Having the GED allows individuals to compete for and obtain better jobs. In addition, as reading levels improve, people become less dependent on social services.

In the Counting on Results Project, for those involved in a literacy program, more than 40 percent had become citizens, slightly more than a third were able to read to a child, and about a quarter noted improved basic life skills (see Table 7.3).

Table 7.3. Basic Literacy Outcomes

Outcomes	Percent Selected
Became a citizen	42
Read to a child or helped a child choose a book	36
Wrote a letter, postcard, or e-mail	28
Managed personal finances better	27
Participated in a community activity	27
Obtained information about bus, car, education, jobs, money, etc.	25
Applied for a job	14

Adapted from Keith Curry Lance, Marcia J. Rodney, Nicolle O. Steffen, Suzanne Kaller, Rochelle Logan, Kristie M. Koontz, and Dean K. Jue. *Counting on Results: New Tools for Outcome-Based Evaluation of Public Libraries.* Aurora, CO: Bibliographic Center for Research, 2002.

Possible performance measures for a literacy program include the number of individuals in the literacy program, number of individuals attending ESL classes, number of volunteer instruction hours, and number of individuals obtaining their GED certificate.

Assessment: Good. It is a straightforward task to document the use of the literacy program and ESL classes. It is much more difficult to demonstrate a link between use of the literacy program and a reduced need for social services or a better job. One effective approach is to document the success stories of those who have used the literacy program.

Support of Education

A majority of public libraries play an important role in supporting the educational institutions in the community. The library's large and diverse collection of resource materials assists students in completing class assignments and going beyond class requirements to learn more about particular topics of interest. In addition to the more traditional school environments, the library also plays an important role for the growing number of home school and alternative school students. The role of the library in supporting education can be divided into three broad groups: preschoolers and young children, teenagers, and adults.

Preschoolers and Young Children

Most public libraries provide a separate collection of materials for young children and preschoolers. Libraries also typically provide story time programs for preschoolers and summer reading programs for young children. It is not unusual for a public library to devote as much as 25 percent or more of its annual acquisitions budget for children's materials. These story time programs provide a way for families to introduce socialization outside the sphere of the family's influence as well as supporting the importance of reading for pleasure. In some cases, a local library will provide a more formalized and organized group for young children, with planned activities and projects. And teachers often use the library's collection of children's materials for activities within their classrooms.

The need for and the strength of the children's collection and educational support services provided by the public library should be designed to complement the resources available within the local elementary, middle, and high schools located in the community. Strong school library media programs can have a positive impact on the reading scores of students.[4]

Possible performance measures for reading readiness for preschool and young children include the number of children using the library annually, proportion of children with library cards in the community, number of children attending story time sessions, number of young children participating in the summer reading program, and circulation of children's materials.

Teenagers

The library plays an important role in supporting education within the community, especially among teenagers. In addition to providing access to resources that can be used for class assignments, the library also provides study space and meeting rooms for students to collaborate on projects. The student has access to print resources, audiovisual materials, full-text electronic journals, and the

Internet to conduct necessary research. Well-educated students will do well whether they attend college or pursue other avenues for finding a fulfilling career. Some public libraries have had difficulty coping with latchkey kids, who are at the library until they are picked up after their parents get off work. Yet society benefits by the public library providing a safe haven for latchkey kids; they could be involved with property destruction, drug use, or street gangs, which clearly result in higher social costs to society at large.

Possible performance measures for the support of education among teenagers are the number of students with library cards, frequency of use by students, total circulation by students, number of students assisted at the reference desk, number of students on class visits to the library, and frequency of Internet use.

Adults

The availability of information resources at the library allows adults to maintain and improve their job skills. Given the rapid speed of change in the workplace, especially with regard to technology, individuals must upgrade their work and life skills to remain competitive. In addition, it is not unusual for someone to have several different career changes during the course of his or her working life. This individual will need to learn the basic knowledge about the new career to be successful. And the library can play a role in this re-education.

A 2002 survey in England found that while many low-achieving adult learners are using the public library heavily, they do so predominantly for leisure activities and are unaware of the potential of the public library as a learning environment.[5] These low achievers are less likely to return to formal education later in life and are underemployed or unemployed.

Common sense and the literature suggest that it is difficult to identify performance measures for the support of education among adults because a great deal of the use of the library is self-service, and people do not report their success.

Assessment: Fair to good. Depending on the focus of the evaluation (children, teenagers, or adults) it is possible to identify and use some fairly reliable output measures.

Lifelong Learning

Information competent people have learned how to learn. They know how information is organized, how to find information, and how to use information in such a way that others can learn from them. They are people prepared for life-long learning because they can always find the information needed for any task or decision that presents itself.—Palomar College Library[6]

Often the public library will serve an important role in furthering the education of adults after their formal schooling has been completed. Some have called this desire for independent learning "lifelong learning," and it is an essential service objective for many public libraries. The concept of lifelong learning refers to a constantly evolving set of skills needed to participate in society and the achievement of goals that may be set by an individual. These adults are borrowing self-help and how-to materials to answer specific questions as well as other materials that will enrich their lives. Clearly the library's collection must reflect the needs and interests of its users.

One of the public library's greatest strengths is that it has done a good job of providing physical access to a variety of collection materials. More recently, this access has been complemented by the provision of information technology to the library's users. Yet most public libraries have not identified an effective way to assist users in learning about intellectual access and learning to make informed, critical decisions about the quality, currency, and authoritativeness of information. Information literacy classes are taught in academic and school library settings, but such a class would rarely be offered in a public library venue.

Part of the goal of lifelong learning for public libraries is to recognize that an ecology of libraries exists in people's minds and that the public library must learn how to effectively partner and complement other types of libraries that exist nearby, be they school, academic, or special libraries.[7]

It would not be too difficult to identify and track the use of the self-help and how-to materials in a public library. (It would be possible to identify call number ranges for such materials and produce a quarterly report of the borrowing and in-library use of such materials, using for example the methodology used in the Counting on Results Project.) In addition, the use of an item may be to meet an information need for a class assignment, required for work, or simply the desire on the part of an individual to satisfy an innate curiosity regarding a particular topic.

Assessment: Difficult.

Local History and Genealogy

Some public libraries are closely connected to their community's historical society and thus provide access to a variety of resources reflecting local history and genealogy. It is not unusual for a library to provide a guide on conducting genealogical searches using such resources as birth and death records from local newspapers, census data, and directories. Availability of computer technology also allows for searching of resources via the Internet.

Users of local history and genealogy resources, as reported in the Counting on Results Project report, found the resources to be helpful and led to positive events in their lives (see Table 7.4).

Table 7.4. Local History and Genealogy Outcomes

Outcomes	Percent Selected
Made progress researching family history	53
Identified new source of information to search	50
Obtained a document or record	42
Shared data with others in person, in print, or online	35
Learned about my community and local history	30
Met others interested in local history or genealogy	28
Learned how to use genealogical databases	22
Learned about cultural heritage	19

Adapted from Keith Curry Lance, Marcia J. Rodney, Nicolle O. Steffen, Suzanne Kaller, Rochelle Logan, Kristie M. Koontz, and Dean K. Jue. *Counting on Results: New Tools for Outcome-Based Evaluation of Public Libraries.* Aurora, CO: Bibliographic Center for Research, 2002.

Potential measures might include output measures indicating the use of available resources, as well as attendance at classes and programs.

Assessment: Difficult.

Social Interactions or Library As Place

In many communities the public library plays an important role in facilitating and encouraging social interactions within the community. The library provides a pleasant and inviting place for reading and individual study, small group rooms for meetings and study, as well as larger meeting rooms and auditoriums. The library may organize forums for the discussion of books (in some cases a booktalk with the author of the book) as well as film series and live performances. Community bulletin boards, of declining interest in recent years for many libraries, may still play a central role in rural public libraries, although this material is often found posted on a library's Web site.

Parents are likely to encourage their children to visit the library since it is perceived as a safe-haven and a place where children can work on their homework and explore personal interests.[8]

Some public libraries also reach out to the community through the use of bookmobiles, books-by-mail, and depository collections in senior centers and retirement communities. Providing access to technology allows individuals to remain in contact with family, friends, and business acquaintances located in other communities. One manifestation of a local library's importance within a community is the fact that friends and neighbors often meet at the library.

As noted in the Counting on Results Project report, the library as place plays an important role within the community. More than two-thirds of respondents indicated that they had learned about new books and other materials (and most likely either borrowed or used the materials in the library) (see Table 7.5).

Table 7.5. Library As Place (Commons) Outcomes

Outcomes	Percent Selected
Learned about new books, videos, or music	67
Found a quiet place to think, read, write, or study	59
Enjoyed a lecture, concert, film, or other public event	26
Completed or made progress on school work	26
Made a new friend	20

Adapted from Keith Curry Lance, Marcia J. Rodney, Nicolle O. Steffen, Suzanne Kaller, Rochelle Logan, Kristie M. Koontz, and Dean K. Jue. *Counting on Results: New Tools for Outcome-Based Evaluation of Public Libraries*. Aurora, CO: Bibliographic Center for Research, 2002.

Potential performance indicators of the library's role in promoting social interactions are the number of individuals served by outreach programs, number of programs offered, and number of people attending programs.

Assessment: Difficult. Despite the ready availability of possible performance measures, it is very difficult to demonstrate the importance of the public library to the vibrancy of social interaction within a community.

Community Awareness

The public library can play a role in assisting various organizations within the community to inform the citizens about upcoming cultural, educational, and recreational events and activities. A number of users make the assumption that their local library, which is "information central," will have information and flyers about upcoming events. In some cases the library may provide display space for flyers and exhibits that focus on a particular theme or activity of interest to the community.

Some public libraries have been actively involved in creating and maintaining a database of community organizations that provide a wide variety of services. As such these public libraries become more closely connected to their community and become a part of a community network. Joan Durance and Karen Fisher-Pettigrew completed an Institute of Museum and Library Services (IMLS)-funded project to assess the impact that this type of activity has within the community.[9] They report that positive personal and family benefits, improved connections to people and groups, and contributions to neighborhood improvements arise from the use of community networks.

Some local libraries are also affiliated with the local historical group and thus provide space and services for a local history collection, genealogy information, and archival materials. The library may use volunteers to produce an index to local newspapers and other projects that will capture local history.

Assessment: Difficult. It is difficult to conceive of a reasonable way to construct performance measures demonstrating community awareness, although it is possible to identify the use of some community resources such as Web-based bulletin boards.

Support for a Democratic Society

Clearly one crucial role for the public library is to provide free access to everyone to a wide variety of information resources. This access to information encourages the individual's participation in democratic institutions and improves the quality of life for all. Such participation can range from informed conversation and discussion, to participation in local government meetings, to voting. Such a vital role is almost impossible to quantify or measure in a valid manner.

Public libraries collect, provide access to, and disseminate government information ranging from statistics, speeches, and drafts of proposed legislation to copies of reports. In addition, some public libraries have special collections of information produced and provided by various government agencies.

Potential performance indicators for the library's role of supporting a democratic society are use of the government documents collection; identifying use of specific portions of the collection; and attendance at booktalks, community forums, and discussions on pertinent topics.

Assessment: Difficult. Other than focusing on the important role of public libraries in supporting a democratic society, there is little that a library can do to demonstrate its contribution in this area.

The Social Audit

The British Library financed several research projects to examine the utility of using a social audit as a potential tool in assessing the social and economic impacts of public libraries.[10] Notable among the final reports was a project conducted by Rebecca Linley and Bob Usherwood.[11] A social audit is a means of assessing the social impact of an organization in relation to its aims and those of its stakeholders. The team conducting the social audit will contact and identify the needs of library nonusers.

Linley and Usherwood used a "social process audit,"[12] which basically collects information through the use of interviews and focus groups with stakeholders. When conducting a social audit, the main criterion for evaluation is the impact of policy on social need, which raises the obvious questions, what constitutes social need, and what is the public library's responsibility in meeting some portion of a social need?[13]

The results of the social audit suggest that the library's *established roles* (culture, education, reading and literacy, and information) have an enduring relevance:

- The library is a center of cultural life.
- Library services support both adults' and children's educational needs.
- The library supports the development of children's reading skills.
- The library is a suitable "nonstigmatized" place for adult literacy classes.
- The library remains important as a source of *free* reading material, especially for people with low economic means.

The public library also has a *social and caring role:*

- Individuals gain new skills and confidence from using the library.
- The library is a place where people meet and share interests, sometimes described as "part of the cement in the social fabric."
- Library promotes greater understanding between different cultural groups.
- The library sustains local identity by developing and maintaining community self-esteem.

The findings of a social audit are derived from qualitative, often anecdotal, evidence and suggest that public libraries enrich the lives of many people. Proponents of the social audit process suggest that use of this technique is what makes the enriching process visible. Opponents of the social audit technique point to the lack of any objective or quantitative performance measures to support the conclusions made as a result of the audit.

In a review of 11 projects that were attempting to assess the social impact of public libraries, Barbara Debono created a list of 15 potential social impacts and noted the number of studies that addressed each potential social impact.[14] The results are shown in Table 7.6.

Table 7.6. Library Social Impacts

Social Impact	Number of Projects
Information literacy	1
Local history/genealogy	1
Develop IT skills	1
Support democracy	1
Culture and arts	3
Increased quality of life	4
Equity/free access	4
Personal development	4
Vocational/economic effects	5
Recreation	5
Community building	6
Decreasing social isolation	6
Education	7
Health and general information	7
Public space	7

Summary

Placing a strong emphasis on the social benefits of public libraries has a strong emotional appeal both for library professionals and for library stakeholders. However, as noted in this chapter, it is difficult to find measures that go beyond the counting of activities. In short, it is challenging to find a link between positive outcomes for an individual or the community and specific library services. And without this causal link the claims of social benefits that arise from the use of the public library are just that—claims.

Notes

1. Barbara Debono. Assessing the Social Impact of Public Libraries: What the Literature Is Saying. *Australasian Public Libraries and Information Services*, 15 (2), June 2002, 80–95.

2. Keith Curry Lance, Marcia J. Rodney, Nicolle O. Steffen, Suzanne Kaller, Rochelle Logan, Kristie M. Koontz, and Dean K. Jue. *Counting on Results: New Tools for Outcome-Based Evaluation of Public Libraries*. Aurora, CO: Bibliographic Center for Research, 2002; see also Nicolle O. Steffan, Keith Curry Lance, and Rochelle Logan. Time to Tell the Whole Story: Outcome-Based Evaluation and the Counting on Results Project. *Public Libraries*, July/August 2002, 222–28; Nicolle O. Steffan and Keith Curry Lance. Who's Doing What: Outcome-Based Evaluation and Demographics in the Counting on Results Project. *Public Libraries*, September/October 2002, 271–79.

3. Catherine Ross. Finding Without Seeking: What Readers Say About the Role of Pleasure Reading As a Source of Information. *Australasian Public Libraries & Information Services*, 13 (3), June 2000, 72–80.

4. Keith Curry Lance, Marcia J. Rodney, and Christine Hamilton-Pennell. *How School Librarians Help Kids Achieve Standards: The Second Colorado Study*. San Jose, CA: Hi Willow Research & Publishing, 2000.

5. Richard Proctor and Craig Bartle. *Low Achievers, Lifelong Learners: An Investigation into the Impact of the Public Library on Educational Disadvantaged*. Library and Information Commission Research Report 117. London: Resource—The Council for Museums, Archives and Libraries, 2002.

6. Palomar College Library. *Why Do We Need Information Competency?* Available at: http://daphne.Palomar.edu/Library/infocomp/whyic.htm (accessed June 16, 2003).

7. Ray Doiron. Lifelong Libraries for Lifelong Learning. *Feliciter*, 46 (1), November 1 2000, 20–24.

8. Glen E. Holt. As Parents and Teachers See It: The Community Values of a Public Library. *The Bottom Line*, 10 (1), 1997, 32–35.

9. Joan C. Durrance and Karen E. Fisher-Pettigrew. Toward Developing Measures of the Impact of Library and Information Services. *Reference & User Services Quarterly*, 42 (1), Fall 2002, 43–53.

10. See, for example, Evelyn Kerslake and Margaret Kinnel. *The Social Impact of Public Libraries: A Literature Review*. British Library Research and Innovation Centre Report 201. London: Community Development Foundation, 1997.

11. Rebecca Linley and Bob Usherwood. *New Measures for the New Library: A Social Audit of Public Libraries*. British Library Research and Innovation Centre Report 89. London: British Library Board, 1998.

12. D. H. Blake, W. C. Frederick, and M. S. Myers. *Social Auditing: Evaluating the Impact of Corporate Programmes*. New York: Praeger, 1976.

13. Janie Percy-Smith. Auditing Social Needs. *Policy and Politics*, 20 (1), 1992, 29–34.

14. Barbara Debono. Assessing the Social Impact of Public Libraries: What the Literature Is Saying. *Australasian Public Libraries and Information Services*, 15 (2), June 2002, 80–95.

Chapter

Economic Impacts

8

One of the primary benefits arising from the use of a library in a corporate or governmental setting is that individuals are able to save time (substitute librarian's time for the user's time). However, the value of time for public library users is something that must be ignored—even if the library user does save time as a result of a library visit. From the perspective of the public library, the community at large is not able to benefit from this time saving on an individual basis. Yet the public library does have a broad and positive economic impact on the community.

As a publicly funded organization, a public library embodies three economic concepts:

- **Merit goods:** goods or services to which society accepts that everyone should have access, regardless of means. Public libraries exhibit some merit properties because they help to maintain literacy, inform and empower citizens, stimulate the imagination, and so forth.

- **Public goods:** goods which, even when consumed by another person, are still available for use by another. An item borrowed from the library's collection, once returned to the library, is available for use by another person.

- **External benefits:** occur when others, not directly involved in a transaction, nevertheless receive benefit from it. For example, a student uses the library to complete an assignment that ultimately leads to a more qualified individual. This individual is able to achieve higher career goals and rely less on government-provided support services.

A survey of library users in Florida found support for the statements that the public library

131

- contributes to the prosperity of the local/state economy (74 percent agree, 17 percent somewhat agree),

- provides economic benefits to local businesses (56 percent agree, 26 percent somewhat agree), and

- contributes to the financial well-being of individuals (54 percent agree, 20 percent somewhat agree).[1]

These library users also felt that the presence of the public library helps attract new businesses to the community, the availability of library resources made them more productive at work, the library assists with issues concerning community development, and the library increased local property values. Yet these are strictly the perceptions of patrons and library directors and do not represent a methodology that would actually calculate the actual benefits in terms of *dollars and cents*.

Generally speaking, it is possible to separate the economic benefits that arise from a public library into two categories: direct and indirect. Charles McClure and his colleagues have suggested that it is possible to think of a "matrix of economic benefits" that arise due to public libraries, as shown in Table 8.1.

Table 8.1. Matrix of Economic Benefits

Nature of Benefit	Class of Beneficiary		
	Individual	*Local Business*	*Local Community*
Direct	Specific economic benefits that accrue to the individual, e.g., cost of borrowing versus buying materials	Specific economic benefits that accrue to local businesses, e.g., custom mailing lists	Specific economic benefits that accrue to the local community, e.g., tax base from library employment
Indirect	General economic benefits that accrue to the individual, e.g., increased property values	General economic benefits that accrue to local businesses, e.g., literate workforce	General economic benefits that accrue to the local community, e.g., quality of life factors

Adapted from Charles R. McClure, Bruce T. Fraser, Timothy W. Nelson, and Jane B. Robbins. *Economic Benefits and Impacts from Public Libraries in the State of Florida: Final Report to State Library of Florida, Division of Library and Information Services*. Tallahassee: Information Use Management and Policy Institute, Florida State University, January 2001, 4–5.

An alternative approach is to identify economic benefits using four different methodologies: cost-benefit analysis, economic impact (contribution of actual dollars to the local community by the library), subsidies the public library provides through its services to other organizations in the community, and cost avoidance (a service provided by the public library need not be duplicated by other private or government agencies).[2]

Direct Benefits for the Individual

Possible direct economic benefits for an individual include

- savings from the nonpurchase of books, magazines, and newspapers;
- information services to personal investors;
- technology access;
- health information; and
- employment information and services.

Savings from the Sharing Rather Than Purchasing of Books, Magazines, and Newspapers

The public library allows many individuals to share library resources, reducing an individual's expenditures (and collectively the community's expenditures) on books, magazines, newspapers, audiotapes, videotapes, and so forth. This freed-up discretionary income will then be spent, and a portion may be spent in the local community.

One way to estimate this economic impact is to determine the average number and type of materials borrowed by an individual on an annual basis. This information, coupled with the average purchase price for each type of material, would then result in an estimate of the savings that would accrue to the individual. Please note, however, that most people would not purchase all of the materials borrowed from the library if the library were no longer available.

Assessment: Easy. It is a straightforward task to estimate the potential savings for the users of these materials based on their subscription costs and the number of users.

Information Services to Personal Investors

Individuals wishing to make informed decisions about their investments can find a wealth of materials about investments at their local public library, ranging from books and magazines to financial newsletters and reports. Among the more popular financial publications are the *Wall Street Journal, Barron's, Business Week*, and *Value Line Investment Survey*. Few individuals can afford to subscribe to this variety of materials pertaining to personal financial planning and thus turn to the library for information about mutual funds, stocks, bonds, and other potential investments and portfolio management.

Possible performance measures pertaining to library services to personal investors include total holdings providing personal financial advice, total in-library use and circulation of such materials, and customer satisfaction regarding the availability of financial materials.

Assessment: Good to very good. Tracing the services used by individuals for personal investment information as well as their satisfaction with the materials provided is a good way to demonstrate value.

Technology Access

The public library can provide access to computers, printers, and the Internet. In addition, the library may offer classes so that individuals can learn new skills or enhance an existing technology-related skill. It is not unusual for a library to offer classes pertaining to basic computer skills, e-mail functions, word processing, spreadsheets, navigating the Internet, and use of Internet search engines.

This technology access is particularly important for a group within any community that cannot afford to purchase computers or pay the monthly service charge to gain access to the Internet. Several studies have demonstrated that lower socioeconomic status is associated with lower levels of access to and use of computers and the Internet; this is sometimes referred to as the "digital divide."[3] Internet access is also of value to visitors in the community who may wish to check their e-mail or perform other computer-based activities.

Obviously providing such a service requires that the library have the necessary computer and communications network infrastructure in place. It also requires training staff to become knowledgeable in technology-related areas to teach classes, respond to questions, and resolve problems. Some libraries have found that using volunteers as teachers and trainers can be an effective alternative to relying solely on library staff members.

A 2003 survey found that the 'digital divide' between rich and poor children is rapidly shrinking as youngsters of all income levels and ethnic groups increasingly use the Internet.[4] Yet there clearly is a need for public libraries to provide access to computer-based technology and the Internet.

Assessment: Good to very good. It is relatively easy to track the number of individuals who use the computers as well as the number of people who attend classes.

Health Information

The public library provides access to a wealth of health-related information. Whether the information is to be found within the library's collection or is accessible via an electronic database or an Internet site, health information can have a profound impact on the lives of individuals or their families. Whether an individual is seeking general information about wellness, fitness, or diet, or is looking for specific information about a disease, treatment, or prescription drugs, the quality and timeliness of the information is of utmost importance.

Assessment: Good to very good. It is possible to track usage of health information resources within the library. Libraries can also ask customers to comment on the value and utility of the health information they have found at the public library.

Employment Information

The public library provides a wide range of information resources pertaining to resumes, developing interviewing skills, career requirements, civil service test requirements, and so forth. Some public libraries not only provide access to relevant materials but also provide programs that focus on practical information and developing skills that will be of value to the participants.[5]

In addition to library materials related to employment and development of job skills, a large number of public libraries provide access to computers and the Internet. Individuals can prepare and update their resumes, look for job wanted listings, and post resumes at Internet job-related Web sites.

A national survey of job and career centers located in public libraries found that people who availed themselves of the centers[6]

- had increased their understanding of the career possibilities,
- were able to make more informed decisions,
- took more positive steps to gain employment,
- gained self-esteem, and
- developed new skills.

Potential performance measures for employment and job-related services provided by the public library include in-library use and circulation of job search materials and career development, number of individuals attending employment/job skills programs, number of people who use the computers for job-related activities, and requests for employment and job-related information at the reference desk. Some libraries have established a dedicated area that provides resources and services to assist people in upgrading their skills and finding jobs.[7]

Assessment: Fair. Although it is relatively easy to track the use of employment-related materials as well as the number of individuals who use the computers or attend programs, it is difficult to assert a causal link between the use of such materials and an individual being hired for a job or reduced unemployment in a community.

Direct Benefits for Local Business

Possible direct economic benefits for local businesses include

- information services to local business and
- economic development.

Information Services to Local Business

The public library will more than likely provide information resources and services that will be of interest to the self-employed in small or home-based businesses as well as to larger companies. The library may be the only affordable and available source of quality information for these individuals and organizations. The topical information sought by small businesses includes marketing (identification of potential customers), technology, management skills, selling/motivation, and possible suppliers.[8]

The information that is provided may be a response to a reference request or use and circulation of business-related periodicals, books, and reports. A wide range of information is used to ensure compliance with government regulations and procedures, developing a marketing plan, product development, creating a business plan, and so forth. Some public libraries develop specialized services for local businesses, which seem to engender real support.[9]

The survey of users of the public library for business and career information, as noted in the Counting on Results Project report, found that the library was a source of information that was helpful in starting and developing a business (see Table 8.2).

Table 8.2. Business and Career Information Outcomes

Outcomes	Percent Selected
Explored/started/developed a business	36
Developed job-related skills	31
Explored job/career or determined necessary education/ training	28
Made better investment or retirement decisions	26
Learned how to advance in job/career	15

Adapted from Keith Curry Lance, Marcia J. Rodney, Nicolle O. Steffen, Suzanne Kaller, Rochelle Logan, Kristie M. Koontz, and Dean K. Jue. *Counting on Results: New Tools for Outcome-Based Evaluation of Public Libraries*. Aurora, CO: Bibliographic Center for Research, 2002.

One large survey found that public libraries are used an average of seven times per year by professionals for work-related purposes.[10] One survey of small business owners found that about one-third used the library frequently and were interested in finding information about consumer markets, technology, and management skills.[11] Yet for many other small business people the library is not even on the radar screen! One study identified the main sources of information for small business and found the following:[12]

Personal contacts	46%
(colleagues, employees, friends, clients, customers)	
Magazines	30%
Newspapers	13%
Manufacturers	13%
Organizations	9%
Directories	8%
Libraries	2%
Advertising	2%

Potential performance measures might include output measures (number of users who use the library for work or a business-related purpose, circulation of business-related books and periodicals, and so forth) as well as developing an estimate of the value of library information to individuals for business purposes (user estimates of time saved, money saved, value of information if purchased elsewhere). A customer satisfaction survey would also reveal the value as perceived by those who use the business-related information.

Assessment: Good to very good. Tracking the services received by individuals for business-related information is an important first step in determining the value of the library for this community of users. This can be followed up with a brief survey to determine the satisfaction of users.

Economic Development

The public library can become the hub or source of information about the community and requirements for establishing a business or enterprise. The information may range from zoning regulations, to availability of land or office space meeting certain requirements, to availability of training programs. In addition, the library's collection will contain information resources pertaining to starting a business, writing a business plan, creating a corporation, and so forth. In some cases, the library may create a specialized business reference service to provide more business-focused information services. Some libraries have developed a tier of business-related reference services in which a business or organization can pay for various levels of service of reference and on-demand information services. Small entrepreneurial business startups are an important segment of our economy, and the public library can play an important role in the fostering of their success.

It is important to ensure that any specialized business-related service is not duplicating an existing publicly funded organization or service. It is recommended that the public library develop a partnership to assist with economic development activities with such organizations as the chamber of commerce or an economic development office.[13]

Possible performance measures include circulation/use of materials focused on starting a business, number of users/businesses that rely on the library for information, and willingness of firms to pay for a premium business-related information service.

Assessment: Limited value. Clearly it would be difficult to track the role of the public library' in the success or failure of new business startups.

Direct Benefits for the Local Community

Possible direct economic benefits for the local community include

- the library as an employer,
- purchase of goods and services,
- retail sales due to the library being a "destination."

The Library As an Employer

The public library is an employer, and providing jobs has a direct economic impact on the community. It can also be argued that some portion of the wages earned by the library staff members are spent in the local community and thus has a positive impact on the local economy. Sometimes this impact is called an "economic multiplier." For example, a dollar spent locally may generate "x" number of dollars in the local economy. A large portion of the public funds invested in the library are committed to employment, and these dollars are "recycled" in the local economy.

Typically the public library will employ women and students as both full-time and part-time employees, which provides both a source of income as well as job skills training to these individuals.

The possible performance measures include salaries paid to full- and part-time employees and number of full- and part-time employees.

Assessment: Limited value. Obviously the economic benefits associated with library employment might also be realized if the public funds were spent on other programs. Thus, this economic benefit of employment is one that is generally not persuasive to local decision makers.

Purchase of Goods and Services

Each year the library purchases materials to add to its collection. Some portion of these purchases may be made locally as opposed to using a national book wholesaler. In addition, the library will purchase goods and services locally that support the local economy. Although it occurs infrequently, the library may build a new building or expand an existing building. Such capital projects contribute to the local economy through employment and the purchase of building materials and services. The flip side of this approach is that most materials purchased for the library's collection are made using vendors not located locally.

Possible performance measures include the total value of purchases in the local community, number of local firms from which goods and services are purchased, and value of construction and renovation of libraries.

Assessment: Limited value.

Retail Sales

An economic impact analysis is used to demonstrate the value that an institution has to the local or regional economy. Such an analysis starts with the fact that the institution attracts new dollars to the community. This analysis is typically used by a major museum or large library, for example, the Art Institute of Chicago, the Natural History Museum of Chicago, the Museum of Modern Art in New York, The New York Public Library, the Library of Congress, and the Huntington Library in San Marino, California. Such well-known institutions as these serve as a "destination" for visitors. While visiting the museum or large library the visitors stay in area hotels, eat at local restaurants, and shop at various stores. The net effect is a boost to the local economy. In addition to the direct dollars spent by visitors, these dollars also cause the employment of other individuals. This spillover effect on the local economy is sometimes called the "multiplier effect."

The public library may be a "destination" or the reason for a trip from the home, school, or business. An individual may combine the visit to the library with other activities, including shopping at nearby stores and restaurants. If library users are from outside the community and shop at nearby stores, this activity will benefit the local economy directly and potentially the tax base for the local jurisdiction in the form of increased sales tax revenues. To demonstrate the connection between use of the library and shopping at nearby stores, a survey would have to be conducted. It would be important to demonstrate a cause-and-effect relationship between the library (the reason for the trip) and the shopping that was done at nearby stores and restaurants. To be effective, it must be demonstrated that the customer has a choice of where to shop and that the library attracts some nonresident individuals who combine shopping with a visit to the library.

When the Hamilton Public Library in Ontario, Canada, introduced a non-resident user fee, the library experienced a reduction in the number of annual visits to the library, to such an extent that parking revenues dropped more than was generated by the library's nonresident user fee.[14] Another public library found that nonresident users of the library spent an average of $24 on each visit.[15]

Only some public libraries will have the collections or other resources to serve as a destination for visitors. Thus, the economic impact approach is one that is suited to partially demonstrating the value of the local public library. This is a measure that must be used in conjunction with other performance measures.

Potential performance measures include the number of nonresidents with library cards, average number of visits to the library by nonresidents, proportion of nonresidents who shop at local stores, and average expenditures attributed to these nonresidents.

Assessment: Limited value. Given the time, resources, and cost to create and administer an economic impact survey, the benefits of such an approach do not appear to justify the effort.

Attracting Industrial and Commercial Development

Businesses looking to locate in a community will look at a wide variety of factors, including the availability of land and buildings to meet their needs, appropriate zoning, tax incentives from the local or state governments, a qualified labor force, proximity to markets and suppliers, and the quality of life in the community. In addition to the quality of schools and recreational and cultural opportunities, the availability of a high-quality public library plays an important role in assessing the quality of life.[16] Given two or more sites where all other factors are equal, the perception of the quality of life in a community is often the deciding factor about where to locate a business. Robert McNulty, a quality of life advocate, suggests that the "economics of amenity" will increase the economic value within a community.[17] A good public library may be an important selling point for a community trying to attract retirees.

The difficulty with this approach to demonstrating the value of the public library is that rarely will the presence of a high-quality public library be the single factor in determining the quality of life for a community. Rather, the perception of the quality of life or a quality of life measure is based on a wide range of factors.

Assessment: Limited value. Obviously it would be difficult to track the role of the public library in attracting industry or commercial firms to the community.

Cost-Benefit Analysis

A cost-benefit analysis can be prepared when the value of a product or service can be expressed in monetary terms and compared with its cost. The cost-benefit methodology is routinely used by corporations to make financial investment decisions and has also been used effectively to evaluate the benefits of education, local government services, social services, and environmental protection programs provided by nonprofit organizations and government agencies.

Cost-benefit analysis suffers from a persistent and difficult problem. Typically the costs of a project or organization are clearly understood and occur in a very specific time period (a one-year budget cycle), whereas the benefits (usually much more difficult to quantify) are spread out over a longer period of time.

There are five possible methods for preparing a cost-benefit analysis and the different approaches can yield different results.[18] The choice of the most appropriate cost-benefit analysis method depends on the situation. Four of these cost-benefit methodologies are designed to assist in making investment decisions: maximize benefits for a given cost, minimize costs for a given level of benefits, maximize the net benefits, and maximize the internal rate of return or return on investment (ROI). These methods are not appropriate for assessing the benefits of public library services and will be ignored in this book. Instead, the focus here is on an approach typically used to assess the value of all library services: identifying the ratio of benefits over costs.

The process of this calculation is straightforward. All of the costs and benefits are identified and expressed as the ratio of benefits to costs, for example, $16 worth of benefits for every $1 of costs or 16:1.

A cost-benefit analysis can measure the direct benefits that accrue to those who have access to the services being measured. The library provides reading and information materials and services directly to its users. These users benefit directly from the use of those services and materials. The St. Louis Public Library tested the use of several cost-benefit methodologies to determine the best approach to valuing the direct benefits of use of the public library. Although a range of benefit values was calculated, in general it was concluded that St. Louis Public Library users derived more than $4 in benefits for each dollar spent.[19]

The cost-benefit methodologies used by the St. Louis Public Library include *consumer surplus*. This approach measures the value that consumers place on the consumption of a good or service in excess of what they must pay to get it. And although library services are "free" (ignoring for a moment that the public library is supported by tax revenues), library users must make a payment by the effort they exert and the time they spend to access library services. A telephone survey was used to determine the number of books borrowed from the library, number of books purchased, and number of additional books they would purchase if they could not borrow materials from the library. The library then created a price for the market substitute for each library service, as shown in Table 8.3 (page 142). The value of borrowing was thus established.

Table 8.3. Pricing of Substitute Market Services

Service	Substitute	Price (in $)	Source
Children's books (paperback)	Bookstore	8.00	*Bowker Annual*
Books for adults (paperback)	Bookstore	14.00	*Bowker Annual*
Video/DVD films	Rental	4.00	Blockbuster Video
Audio/music	Purchase	13.00	WalMart
Magazines	Newsstand	3.00	Local newsstand
Newspapers	Newsstand	1.00	Local newsstand
Toys	Educational Store	15.00	Local educational store
Reference and research services	Information Broker	50.00 /hour	Information broker
Special events	Cultural Center	9.00	Local cultural center
Craft and activity programs	YMCA	1.00 /hour	YMCA
Social skills/ Etiquette training	YMCA	1.00 /hour	YMCA
Computer services	Local Coffee Shop	Free	Local coffee shop
Adult education	Public Schools	Free	Public schools
Family or parenting programs	Public Schools	Free	Public schools
Storytelling programs	Local Bookstore	Free	Local bookstore
Meeting space	Local Public School	Free	Local public school
Encyclopedias	Purchase a CD	75.00	*Encarta*
Dictionaries and almanacs	Local Bookstore	10.00	Local bookstore

In the case of the St. Louis Public Library, the consumer-surplus methodology produced an estimated value of $168.7 million on an annual library budget of $15.3 million, or the benefits received were more than $10 for each dollar of tax support. Four library services accounted for 94 percent of the total estimated value: reference/research/readers advisor, 40 percent; books for adults, 29 percent; children's books, 13 percent; and electronic media, 12 percent.[20] One of the problems with this particular methodology, as noted by a number of economists, is that what people *are* prepared to pay for is not the same as what people *say* they are prepared to pay for.[21]

An easier and less costly option (a telephone survey is not used) followed by a number of public libraries is to combine their output measures with a fair market value to ascertain the cost-benefit analysis for the library. As shown in Figure 8.1 (page 144), the San Diego Public Library has concluded that benefits exceed costs by a factor of 6:1. The Miami-Dade Public Library System performed a similar calculation and also found a benefit to cost ratio of 6:1, as shown in Table 8.4 (page 145). Obviously each library must determine the appropriate market price for each type of transaction to calculate its own cost-benefit ratio. For example, the library might check the price of renting a video from two or three commercial rental stores.

The business of the public library is to gather books, information, and related material to make them available, **Free** to the residents of the City of San Diego, CA. If our patrons had to buy these materials and services in Fiscal Year 2001 they would have paid at least . . . .
$160,207,881!

For example:

6,587,872 items (including books, audio-visual materials, etc.) were borrowed. At an average retail price of $20, these would have cost **$131,757,540**

1,617,633 books, periodicals and newspapers were used in libraries but not checked out. Had the library user had to purchase these materials at an average retail price of $10 these would have cost **$16,176,330**

1,835,706 questions were answered in person and by telephone by library staff. Had the library user had to pay $2 for each inquiry, the cost would have been **$3,671,412**

308,362 persons used the electronic magazines and newspapers on the library's IAC database. If the user had to purchase these materials or pay for access at $5 each, these activities would be worth **$1,541,810**

536,974 persons signed up and used the Internet on a Library workstation. If the user had to pay for access at $10 each, these activities would be worth **$5,369,740**

154,017 persons attended 4,370 library programs (excluding the film and Chamber Music series). At a $2.50 admission these activities would be worth **$385,034**

22,400 children and teens registered for the Summer Reading Program. If each had paid a $5 registration fee, this would have cost **$110,200**

618 literacy and ESL tutors provided 43,554 hours of tutoring to 839 learners. At $25/hour, this service would have cost **$1,088,850**

227 students spent 6,170 hours using computer resources at the Library's Literacy Computer Lab. At $10/hour, this would have cost **$61,700**

4,853 persons attended Monday evening and Sunday afternoon film series. At a $5 admission, these activities would be worth **$24,285**

2,100 persons attended the Chamber Music series at the Central Library. At $10 admission, these activities would be worth **$21,000**

These are just some of the services the public library provided in FY 2001. The value was much more to many more users than the estimate of $160,207,881. However, all of the library's services in FY 2001 cost the taxpayer of the City of San Diego only $27,675,365.

Figure 8.1. How Much Is Library Service Really Worth?

Table 8.4. Miami-Dade Public Libraries
Estimated Return on Investment, 1998–1999

Materials and Services	Estimated Benefits
4,751,514 books and materials were borrowed; if purchased the average retail price would be $20 each.	$95,030,280
4,614,903 books, periodicals, and newspapers were used in libraries; if purchased the average retail price of each would be $10.	46,149,030
5,435,095 reference questions answered in person by library staff; if the charge were $2 per inquiry:	10,870,190
625,292 Internet sessions at a $2 per session access fee:	1,250,584
420,581 persons attended 8,546 programs and exhibitions; if there were a $2 admission:	841,162
19,000 children and teens participated in the Mayor's Summer Reading Program; if there were a $5 registration fee:	95,000
279 literacy tutors provided 10,015 hours of one-on-one tutoring to 239 Project LEAD participants; if there were a charge of $25/hour:	250,375
Total benefits	$154,486,621
Less taxpayers' investment (annual library budget)	-24,645,113
Total return on investment	**$129,841,508**
Benefit-to-cost ratio	**6.3:1**

The cost savings to library users from borrowing materials (books, books on tape, audiocassettes, videos, CDs, and DVDs) rather than having to buy them is substantial. The cumulative "savings" for each of the individuals borrowing materials can be calculated to demonstrate this value of the public library.

Calculating the cost-benefit ratio allows the public library to communicate to the library's stakeholders the "return on investment" made by the community in its local library. Being able to indicate that the ratio for a particular library is x dollars of benefits ($4 or $6 or $x) for every dollar of the library's budget is an important message to deliver.

This cost-benefit ratio, or return on investment (ROI), is a way to demonstrate to taxpayers and library funding decision makers the value of information services compared with the total annual budget. Such an approach can move the discussion of the library's budget from being a revenue "sinkhole" to one that clearly demonstrates value for each dollar of investment.

One of the problems associated with the use of the cost-benefit ratio as calculated above is that each use of a particular item is treated as if it were a new purchase by the library on behalf of the user. In addition, the material in the library's collection will be there for several years and used with less frequency over time. Clearly material in a library's collection is going to have a value each time it is used, but from an economic viewpoint the value will be less than the original purchase price. A number of studies have attempted to calculate a more realistic value of an item being circulated (used by a library customer) as a percent of the purchase price of the item.

J. P. Newhouse and A. J. Alexander constructed an economic model based on data collected at the Beverly Hills (California) Public Library that suggested that the value of an item being loaned was 10 percent of the purchase price of a book. They concluded that the maximum benefit was derived from books that were issued frequently over a long period of time.[22] A "Value Added Library Methodology" (V+LM) was developed in New Zealand that was based on the assumption of a hypothetical commercial market with willing buyers and sellers that would price the outputs of the service. The result of the New Zealand approach was to use an average book loan value of NZ$7.96 or 25 percent of the average book purchase price.[23]

The V+LM approach was to identify and quantify what the library does that adds value, what activities add the greatest value, whether the budget allocation is appropriate, and any inconsistencies between principles and actions.[24] A library's service is valued with the V+LM methodology using three main measures:

- *Market price proxy,* which estimates the market price in an imagined situation where there is a willing seller and a willing buyer.

- *Replacement cost,* which estimates what it would cost to replace the service.

- *Opportunity cost,* which estimates the value from using a service assuming less time spent on searching for information.

Public, academic, and special libraries have used the V+LM methodology. For example, the Manakau Public Libraries, which has a budget of NZ$12 million, calculated a return to the community of at least NZ$18 million (a 66 percent return on the library's annual budget).

A project in England to estimate the value of public library benefits estimated the value of the loaning of materials and reference services and found that the value of benefits slightly exceeded the costs of providing the service. The project developed a simplified equation to estimate benefits:

$$V = 0.15IP$$

Where V = value; I = circulation of books; and P = the average price of acquiring the book.[25] This formula has the following attributes:

- Books acquired but not loaned will depress the value

- The higher the circulation, the higher the value

- More expensive books have a greater impact on value (the user receives more benefit)

- The value of paperback books is accurately reflected

- Hardback books have a longer lending life than paperbacks

- The formula is simple to use.

Some public libraries have introduced per-use fees, which are prices ranging from 10 to 25 percent of the original purchase price. Another approach would be to determine the prices charged by the few book subscription libraries still in operation. Similarly, some libraries charge a user fee to obtain audiovisual materials. The mean fee as a percent of price among public libraries in England[26] is

Talking books	4%
Audiocassettes	5%
Compact discs	8%
Videocassettes	20%

Although there is no agreement regarding the value of a borrowed item based on the above studies, it would seem prudent to use a conservative value of 10 percent. It is also fair to suggest that users of the public library tend to undervalue in monetary terms their ability to borrow materials from their local library.

Other Cost-Benefit Methodologies

Willingness-to-Pay Approach

The willingness-to-pay approach is a cost-benefit methodology that asks individuals how much they would be willing to pay to have something they currently do not have. People could be asked how much they are willing to pay rather than forego use of the library or, if a public library did not exist, how much they would be willing to pay in taxes to enjoy the library privileges they have today.

In the case of the St. Louis Public Library, the willingness-to-pay methodology produced a 1 to 1 relationship. That is, the individuals in the survey would be willing to pay $1 for every dollar in the current library budget if all libraries were kept open.

A survey in England found that the threshold beyond which the willingness to pay drops dramatically was £1 (about US$1.50).[27] Based on this result, the authors conclude that the value of a book loan is approximately 7 to 8 percent of the price of the book.

Willingness-to-Accept Approach

This cost-benefit methodology, sometimes called *contingent valuation*, asks individuals how much they would be willing to accept to give up something they already have. Specifically, the individuals surveyed were asked how much they would accept to give up library privileges or how much of a tax cut they would accept in exchange for closing all public libraries.

The St. Louis Public Library found that survey respondents indicated that it would take a $7 payback for every dollar in the library's annual budget if the libraries were to close. However, a significant number of respondents (88 percent) refused to answer the question, indicating that the library was too important or too valuable; that the community needed the public library; or that the children or the family needed the public library. To be valid, contingent valuation must be able to measure nonuse values as well as use values, be capable of integrating valuation motives that extend beyond the pursuit of individual self-interest, and not violate the assumption of rationality.[28]

Obviously, circumstances and subjective evaluations are at the heart of the value assessments derived when using either the willingness-to-pay or the willingness-to-accept methodologies. The users' expectations, tasks, purposes, and previous experiences in using the public library will in large part determine their assessment of the value of library services. This is clearly evident on the part of some users who were reluctant or refused to identify a price for library services.[29]

Cost-of-Time Approach

This methodology suggests that library users must expend time and effort to access library services and that the value of their time is at least as great as the value of the public library. The telephone survey asked for the respondent's annual salary. The value for stay-at-home spouses and teenagers was conservatively valued slightly below the minimum wage. The value of young children was valued at zero. Using this methodology, the St. Louis Public Library produced a valuation of $5.50 in value for each dollar of the library budget.[30]

But the funding decision makers for most public libraries will not put much stock in the fact that the library is saving its users time and effort.

Assessment: Limited to moderate value. The problem with using the cost-benefit analysis is that regardless of the methodology chosen, it requires a significant expenditure of time and money to conduct the necessary telephone survey. However, it is possible to use some of the shortcuts identified earlier in this chapter as a good surrogate measure to determine a return on investment for a public library. The use of the cost-benefit approach can easily be used by most public libraries.

Ultimately the library director must make a determination whether an economic analysis such as a cost-benefit analysis will strengthen the public library's position within the community and with the funding decision makers.

> *Due to their organized methods of identifying, locating and retrieving information, libraries save users millions of dollars each year in time not wasted in attempting to recreate data already available, time saved in not duplicating work already done and time not wasted on erroneous work.*—Robert Kraushaar and Barbara Beverly[31]

Indirect Benefits for the Individual

Possible indirect economic benefits for an individual include enhanced property values.

Enhanced Property Values

The residential and commercial properties located near a public library facility may be a factor affecting the value of these properties. The positive impact on the valuation of these properties may then mean increased tax revenues for the local government.[32] The American Association of Certified Appraisers suggests that appraisers determine whether a community has a local library when assessing property values. Obviously there are a large number of factors that affect the valuation of property, and the proximity of a library will likely have both positive and negative components (increased traffic, parking). It might be possible to garner testimonials from local real estate agents about the value of the library and nearby residential property values.

Assessment: Limited value. It would be difficult to establish a relationship between property values and the presence of a nearby library.

Indirect Benefits for Local Business

Potential indirect economic benefits for local business include a literate workforce.

Literate Workforce

Employers are seeking potential employees who are literate and motivated. In some cases, the availability of a wide range of reading materials promotes the goal of supporting "lifelong learning" among the citizens of a community. Given the rapid rate of change in our society in general and with technology in particular, it is important for people to upgrade their skills so that they can remain competitive in the marketplace. It is not surprising that a number of residents will turn to the public library for information resources as they pursue their goals of learning.

Potential performance measures for a library's ability to support lifelong learning include the number of job skills training and development programs offered, number of individuals attending job skills training and development programs, and users' ratings of such programs.

It would be very difficult to track use of particular library materials as they relate to job skills training and development, just as it would be very difficult to identify the causal link between attendance at the library's programs and job promotions, pay raises, or being hired for a new job.

Assessment: Limited value.

Indirect Benefits for the Local Community

Possible indirect economic benefits for the local community include the following:

- a literate workforce;

- a workforce trained in using current information technology;

- encouragement of entrepreneurship is encouraged, to benefit the general economy; and

- a population that is happy with their lives and where they live.

One possible methodology that can be used to demonstrate the indirect economic benefits of a public library is to utilize a variation of the cost-benefit technique. The public library provides users with services from which the users receive direct benefits. Society as a whole receives an indirect benefit as the unemployed are hired and children grow up to be literate workers and informed citizens. Yet the value of these indirect benefits is difficult to identify and estimate. Without a fairly accurate picture of the benefits in quantifiable terms, the cost-benefit methodology cannot be used.

Although some quality of life indexes (*Best Places to Live, Best Places to Retire, Southern California Best Places,* and so forth) use a "books per capita" statistic as one factor among many when rating communities, the reality is that a good quality public library has only a modest impact on the overall rating of a community. Other factors such as crime, recreational opportunities, weather, health, and the environment are much more important in the quality of life ratings and are often 'weighted' to reflect this higher value.

Assessment: Limited value. Due to the problems with estimating the value of indirect or societal benefits associated with a public library, this approach is not recommended.

Summary

As shown in this chapter, it is difficult to ascertain what are the economic benefits that arise from public library utilization in the lives of its users and the cumulative financial impact on the local community. A number of approaches have been suggested and have been used in some cases, but none clearly captures the economic benefits of the public library. The best approach may be to calculate the cost-benefit of the public library using circulation statistics and other outcome measures combined with market prices, as was done by the San Diego and Miami-Dade public libraries. This will enable the library to show the ratio of benefits to costs when communicating with its users and funding stakeholders.

Notes

1. Bruce T. Fraser, Timothy W. Nelson, and Charles R. McClure. Describing the Economic Impacts and Benefits of Florida Public Libraries: Findings and Methodological Applications for Future Work. *Library & Information Science Research*, 24 (3), 2002, 211–33; Charles R. McClure, Bruce T. Fraser, Timothy W. Nelson, and Jane B. Robbins. *Economic Benefits and Impacts from Public Libraries in the State of Florida: Final Report to State Library of Florida, Division of Library and Information Services*. Tallahassee: Information Use Management and Policy Institute, Florida State University, January 2001. A sample of 1,956 user surveys from 120 different public libraries located throughout Florida was analyzed.

2. Jennifer Abend and Charles R. McClure. Recent Views on Identifying Impacts from Public Libraries. *Public Library Quarterly*, 17 (3), 1999, 3–29.

3. Ann P. Bishop, Tonyia J. Tidline, Susan Shoemaker, and Pamela Salela. Public Libraries and Networked Information Services in Low-Income Communities. *Libraries & Information Science Research*, 21 (3), 1999, 361–90.

4. The Corporation for Public Broadcasting. *Connected to the Future: A Report on Children's Internet Use for the Corporation for Public Broadcasting*. Washington, DC: The Corporation for Public Broadcasting, 2003.

5. Robert R. Pankl. Marketing Practical Information. *Public Library Quarterly*, 20 (3), 2001, 41–60.

6. Steve Oserman and Joan C. Durrance. Providing Support for Job Seekers and Career Changers. *RQ*, 33 (3), Spring 1994, 322–25.

7. Norman J. Eriksen and Jan A. Maas. Serving the Patron Through Referral Lists: The Brooklyn Experience. *Journal of Interlibrary Loan, Document Delivery & Information Supply*, 7 (4), 1997, 49–58.

8. I. Q. Vaughan, J. Tague-Sutcliffe, and P. Tripp. The Value of the Public Library to Small Businesses. *RQ: Reference Quarterly*, 36 (2), 1996, 262–69.

9. Kem B. Ellis. The Challenge of Measuring the Economic Impact of Public Library Service. *North Carolina Libraries,* 52, Summer 1994, 52–56; Helen B. Josephine. Fee-Based Services: An Option for Meeting the Information Needs of the Business Community. *Reference Librarian*, 49–50, 1995, 195–203.

10. Jose-Marie Griffiths and Donald W. King. Libraries: The Undiscovered National Resource, in M. Feeney and M. Grieves (Eds.). *The Value and Impact of Information*. London: Bowker & Saur, 1994, 79–116.

11. Vaughan et al. Value of the Public Library to Small Businesses.

12. Anthony Miele and Nancy Welch. Libraries As Information Centers for Economic Development. *Public Libraries*, 34 (1), January/February 1995, 18–22.

13. Stan Skrzeszewski and Maureen Cubberley. Community-Based Economic Development and the Library—A Concept Paper. *Library Management*, 18 (7), 1997, 323–27.

14. K. Roberts. *The Effects of Non-resident User Fees on Central Library Use*. Hamilton, ON: Hamilton Public Library, 1996.

15. Abend and McClure. Recent Views on Identifying Impacts from Public Libraries, 17.

16. Leonard Lund. *Locating Corporate Research and Development Facilities*. New York: The Conference Board, 1986; Jack Lyne. Quality-of-Life Factors Dominate Many Facility Location Decisions, in *Site Selection Handbook*. *Volume 33*, Atlanta, GA: Conway Publications, August 1988; Roger W. Schmenner. *Making Business Location Decisions*. New York: Prentice Hall, 1982; Rob Sawyer. The Economic and Job Creation Benefits of Ontario Public Libraries. *The Bottom Line*, 9 (4), 1996, 14–26.

17. Robert McNulty. The Economics of Amenity. *Meanjin*, 47 (4), Summer 1988, 615–24.

18. John L. King and Edward L. Schrems. Cost-Benefit Analysis of Information Systems Development and Operation. *Computing Surveys*, 10 (1), March 1978, 22–34. For a review of the economics involved in creating a cost-benefit analysis, see Bruce R. Kingma. *The Economics of Information: A Guide to Economic and Cost-Benefit Analysis for Information Professionals*. Englewood, CO: Libraries Unlimited, 2001.

19. Glen E. Holt and Donald Elliott. Proving Your Library's Worth: A Test Case. *Library Journal*, 123 (18), November 1998, 42–44; Glen E. Holt, Donald Elliott, and Christopher Dussold. A Framework for Evaluating Public Investment in Urban Libraries. *The Bottom Line*, 9 (4), Summer 1996, 4–13; Glen E. Holt, Donald Elliott, and Amonia Moore. Placing a Value on Public Library Services: A St. Louis Case Study. *Public Libraries*, 38 (2), March–April 1999, 98+.

20. Holt, Elliott, and Moore. Placing a Value on Public Library Services.

21. James Nathaniel Wolfe with the assistance of Thomas M. Atichison. *Economics of Technical Information Systems*. New York: Praeger, 1974.

22. Joseph P. Newhouse and Arthur J. Alexander. *An Economic Analysis of Public Library Services*. Santa Monica, CA: Rand Corporation, 1972.

23. Library & Information Association of New Zealand. *Manukau Libraries: Trial of the V+LM Value Added Library Methodology*. Trial Report. New Zealand: LIANZA, October 12, 2000.

24. Ruth MacEachern. Measuring the Added Value of Library and Information Services: The New Zealand Approach. *IFLA Journal* 27, (4), 2001, 232–37.

25. John Sumsion, Margaret Hawkins, and Anne Morris. Estimating the Economic Value of Library Benefits. *Performance Measurement and Metrics*, 4 (1), 2003, 13–27.

26. Sheffield Information Organization. *The Impact of Non-fiction Lending from Public Libraries*. Sheffield, England: SINTO, 1999.

27. Anne Morris, Margaret Hawkins, and John Sumsion. Value of Book Borrowing from Public Libraries: User Perceptions. *Journal of Librarianship and Information Science*, 33 (4), December 2001, 191–98.

28. Svanhild Aabo and Ragnar Audunson. Rational Choice and Valuation of Public Libraries: Can Economic Models for Evaluating Non-market Goods Be Applied to Public Libraries? *Journal of Librarianship and Information Science*, 34 (1), March 2002, 5–15.

29. Debora Shaw and Taemin Kim Park. Comparing Users' Exchange Values with Library Costs in Academic and Public Libraries. *Proceedings of the ASIS Annual Meeting*, 31, 1994, 51–53.

30. Holt, Elliott, and Moore. *Placing a Value on Public Library Services*. St. Louis: St. Louis Public Library, 1998. Available at: http://www.slpl.lib.mo.us/libsrc/restoc.htm (accessed June 16, 2003).

31. Robert Krashaar and Barbara Beverly. Library and Information Services for Productivity. *The Bookmark*, 48, Spring 1990, 167.

32. Jeffrey M. Cooper and Marilyn C. Crouch. Benefit Assessment Helps Open Doors of One Cash-Strapped California Library. *American Libraries,* 25, March 1994, 232–34.

Chapter

Putting It All Together

Sometimes what counts can't be counted, and what can be counted doesn't count.—Albert Einstein[1]

Because libraries engage in many activities that can be easily counted, librarians have tended to focus on quantities of use as indicators of the goodness of the service.—Peter Hernon and Ellen Altman[2]

One of the real ironies of life for public libraries is that the library's stakeholders and citizens of the community have no real clear idea of what constitutes a quality library. Since most people will say that their public library is good, how then are a library director and the management team of a library going to communicate how the library is actually doing and what it would really take in the way of financial resources to change a library so that it could be providing "top notch" quality library services? And how can they identify and then communicate the improvements in existing library services if the library's budget were to be increased by 10 percent, 25 percent, or more?

Part of the problem confronting a public library is that it needs to tackle a range of barriers, be they attitudes, expectations, beliefs, or knowledge and personal experience, that exist in the minds of its stakeholders: users, nonusers, and community decision makers. Some believe that going to the library is too time-consuming, others have difficulty finding their way around the library to the desired resources, while others find the atmosphere of the library uncomfortable and staid. And although almost everyone will appraise the public library quite highly, a quarter of nonusers rate the library unfavorable and another third rate it as neutral.[3] In addition, some segments of the community are ignorant of all the available public library services.

155

Ask anyone what comes to mind when you say "library" or "librarian" and immediately a surfeit of stereotypes springs to mind. Nevertheless, selected stereotypes of the library and librarian can be used in a positive manner to improve the image of the library in the community if a creative, effective communications program is put into place.

> *Public libraries operate on a minimum level of user satisfaction, surviving largely on good will, low expectations and relatively easy demands of the majority of users.*—Barry Totterdell and Jean Bird[4]

The public library is an institution replete with conflicting perceptions, including the following:

- Appreciated and cherished by many users and viewed with indifference or ignorance by others.

- Well-liked as viewed by use of the materials in its collection, yet saddled with an image as a somewhat "stuffy" place.

- Focused on providing equal access to resources and services yet weighed down by a controlling, bureaucratic staff.

- Modern in some respects and clinging to the past in other communities.

- Pledged to provide friendly customer service yet staffed by employees who, in some cases, have poor "people skills."

- Providing a safe, welcoming environment yet having to cope with antisocial behavior on the part of some individuals.

- Free yet charging for some services (and the rationale for charging for what services and how much seems to have no rhyme nor reason).

- Historically focused on the printed word yet providing access to audiovisual materials, the latest information technology, and electronic resources.

- Providing access to electronic resources from the library (yet some do not consider providing access to users located remotely a "library service").

- Focused on controlling the library's collection yet confronted with providing access to chaos (the Internet).

- Counting number of items borrowed or downloaded, which may be irrelevant to performance.

- Providing an amalgamation of various services yet having to identify a "suite" of measures that reflect total performance.

- Increasingly as we move to access of networked information resources, not in control of the response times experienced by users.

- Designed to provide users with access to the collection for "self-service" yet forcing users who are ill equipped to determine when it would be fruitful to ask for assistance.

- Financially well supported in some areas but the very "poor relation" in other communities.

- Controlled by funding decision makers who rarely visit the library.

- Willing to embrace new services yet unwilling to eliminate any existing infrequently used service.

If someone decides to use the library there are a number of barriers that must be negotiated, including:[5]

- *Price to the user.* Price is defined as the cost to the user in terms of time, effort, and money. The most precious resource that an individual has is time and attention. The fact that an individual chooses to use his or her time to visit a public library should be recognized and rewarded.

- *Identification.* Deciding where to look for information and what specific book, cassette, or other material will be best.

- *Cognitive access.* The user must have the cognitive ability or knowledge to find the item in the library as well as to use and understand the material.

- *Availability.* Is the desired item to be found in the library? Should/will the library obtain the item for the user?

- *Acceptability.* Does the material meet such standards as accuracy and credibility?

- *Cost to the library.* Direct costs experienced by the library to provide the desired materials.

> *Trying to manage a library service without the systematic employment of performance measurement could be compared to the experience of Christopher Columbus: when he set sail he did not know where he was going; when he got there he did not know where he was and when he got back he did not know where he had been—and he did it all on someone else's money.*—Jennifer Cram[6]

Culture of Assessment

It would be encouraging to state that a majority of public libraries have developed a "culture of assessment," but such is not the case. The majority of public libraries collect performance measures either because they are mandated or due to tradition. A recent survey of Florida public libraries found that although a wide variety of performance measures were used, library directors felt that their positive impact was limited.[7] Few of these libraries relied on customer satisfaction surveys, most had concerns about the accuracy of measures, and most did not appreciate the value and utility of employing performance measures. Perhaps these library directors felt that the performance measures used in their libraries did not reflect the impact of the public library on the community. As such the data collected are often isolated, sometimes referred to in the literature as "orphaned data," and not related to a planned program of providing performance measures to either the library management team or interested stakeholders.

This lack of a culture of assessment is most distressing since using performance measures in a systematic manner can produce many positive benefits for a library. The collection of data can be the catalyst to move a library in the right direction, make improvements in services to improve productivity and lower costs per transaction, improve customer service, and demonstrate the value of the library to its stakeholders.

> *You can either take action or wait for a miracle to happen. Miracles are great but they are unpredictable.*—Peter Drucker[8]

The data that can be collected by the library include the traditional counts and other numeric values used in the majority of performance measures as well as qualitative data from focus groups, surveys, and benchmarking activities.

In particular, public libraries should shift their inward-looking focus that results from the collection and use of input, process, and output measures to measures that concentrate on the outcomes or impacts on the individual and the community. This outward-looking or customer focus has several implications:[9]

- The most important part of an organization is its customers.
- Attracting new customers and retaining existing customers means you must satisfy their needs.
- The library can't satisfy customers' needs unless you know what their needs are.

In addition, this customer focus means that staff are likely to abandon the perspective of the traditional, and perhaps limiting, departmental boundaries and identify solutions to problems and opportunities that will be most beneficial to the customer.

To achieve the benefits that a "culture of assessment" will bring, Amos Lakos has suggested that

> libraries must have an organizational environment in which decisions are based on facts, research and analysis, and where services are planned and delivered in ways that maximize the positive outcomes and impacts for customers and stakeholders. A culture of assessment exists in organizations where staff care to know what results they produce and how those results related to customer expectations. Organization mission, values, structures and systems support behavior that is performance and learning focused.[10]

There are a number of reasons why a culture of assessment and use of performance measures are not frequently found in a public library, including the following:

- *The perception that you can't measure what the library does.* Clearly it is difficult to assess the impact of the library on its users and its community. But a great many measures have been developed, and with enough creativity and motivation, additional measures will be created.

- *The library does not have total control over the outcomes.* This is true of most government agencies, but it is still possible to demonstrate some measures of outcomes and the impact of the library on the community.

- *Assessment invites unfair comparisons.* A comparison with other libraries is going to happen—period. By taking the initiative, the library can assist in selecting comparable libraries; you can assist in proactively comparing performance that will be beneficial to your library.

- *Such information can be used against the library.* Demonstrating openness and accountability, even when the news is not positive, inspires trust. Being open about what areas need improvement and showing that plans are in place to make enhancements is all that most stakeholders are looking for.

Developing a culture of assessment means providing library staff with the tools and training to prepare assessments. Library staff members should be encouraged to study and chart existing processes and to use process improvement tools and benchmarking. Just as forward-looking organizations are focused on continuous improvement, so too must libraries invest in their staff by providing opportunities for continuous learning. This learning can be formalized using specific training sessions or classes as well as taking advantage of on-the-job training opportunities.

Amos Lakos asserts that it is possible to change libraries so that they move to embrace a culture of assessment. He suggests that a culture of assessment exists when:[11]

- The library's mission, planning, and policies are focused on supporting the customer's information and communication needs, and written documents explicitly acknowledge a customer focus.

- Performance measures are included in library planning documents such as strategic plans. Along with identifying a specific set of measures, a timeframe for achieving targets for each measure is defined.

- Library managers are committed to supporting assessment. Use of assessment tools must be encouraged, and staff at all levels should be encouraged to participate. Assessment must become a part of the normal work process.

- Continuous communication with customers is maintained through needs assessment, quality outcome, and satisfaction measurements.

- All library programs, services, and products are evaluated for quality and impact. The focus of evaluation must include quality assessments as well as the actual outcomes or impacts of the library on the lives of users. It is important for staff to understand that the assessment will focus on the processes, procedures, and services rather than on individuals.

- Staff have the opportunity and resources to improve their skills to better serve users.

More than twenty years ago, Tom Peters and Bob Waterman found that top companies were "measurement-happy and performance-oriented."[12] Since that time there has been an increasing amount of evidence to support their observation about the value of performance measurement. A more recent study found that top performing firms have a clarity of purpose and a vision of the future that is communicated throughout the organization and to interested stakeholders. These firms measured what matters using a variety of metrics.[13]

> *When you cannot measure it, when you cannot express it in numbers, your knowledge is of a meager and unsatisfactory kind.*—Lord Kelvin[14]

> *When you can measure it, when you can express it*
> *in numbers, your knowledge is still of a meager*
> *and unsatisfactory kind.*—Jacob Viner[15]

Evaluation and assessment must become the norm in public libraries. Assessment should be talked about and encouraged in staff meetings. Good assessment requires the active participation of staff at all levels, and different points of view are a foundation for a good culture of assessment. Such an environment allows the library to move from the use of traditional "internally-focused" measures to the use of a combination of measures that will better reveal the value and impact of the public library on its customers. Understanding, communicating, and measuring what matters from the customer's perspective is crucial in making a public library an organization that embraces a culture of assessment. The library must be able to identify and communicate how it adds value to the lives of its users and the quality of life in its community.

One quick way to assess the culture of assessment in your library is to answer the following set of questions. Do the library's managers:

- Articulate a clear vision of the future that inspires employees?
- Maintain consistency between words and actions?
- Maintain consistency between words and actions?
- Know what customers/users really want?
- Encourage the use of performance measures and analysis to assess problems and services?
- Use resources effectively?
- Encourage employees to develop performance measurement skills?
- Demonstrate a constant pursuit of excellence?
- Recruit talented people?
- Learn from their mistakes?
- Seize opportunities when they present themselves?
- Work constantly to improve productivity and eliminate bureaucracy?

Policy-Management Cycle

The policy-management cycle, shown in Figure 9.1 (page 162), illustrates the planning, implementation, and evaluation cycle that a majority of public libraries use each year. Resources are allocated and then converted, using processes and systems, into a service capability. Performance measures are gathered and used in an evaluation process (this process maybe formal or informal), and the results are used to identify areas for improvement.

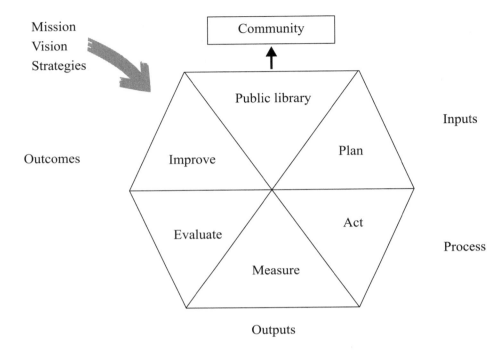

Figure 9.1. Policy-Management Cycle

For most public libraries, this policy-management cycle is pro forma in that the library's funding agency indicates the size of the budget increase or decrease and the library makes the necessary adjustments. For the majority of public libraries the collection of performance measures is also pro forma. That is, statistics and data are gathered, either as required by the state library and/or tradition, but the statistical data are rarely analyzed, and the resulting information about the actual performance of the library and its impact on individuals is not cycled into the policy-management cycle. Such data are sometimes referred to as "orphaned data" or "data silos" since they are not shared and integrated within the organization.

However, with a program that embraces performance measures and assessment, the library can position itself to garner a greater share of resources by communicating the value of the public library directly to its users and to the library's funding decision makers. A combination of input, process, output, and outcome measures can be employed to create a comprehensive picture of the impact of the public library on the lives of individuals and the community's quality of life.

Performance Measures

Performance measurement is not an end in itself but rather a means to improve operations and services and for reporting to various stakeholders. In short, performance measures form a hierarchy, as shown in Figure 9.2. The library can utilize a variety of input, process, output, and outcome or impact performance measures.[16]

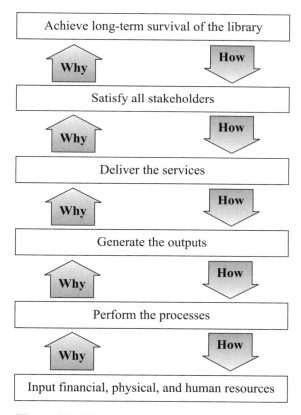

Figure 9.2. Hierarchy of Performance Measures

The key to communicating how effective the public library is within the community is to actively involve the various stakeholders, especially the funding decision makers, in determining what information they would like to know about the library. In particular, asking these individuals what questions about the library they would like answered is very important to gain a better understanding of what issues and perspectives are important to them individually and collectively. With this understanding in hand, it is then possible to identify a set of performance measures that will have maximum impact.

Neil McLean and Clare Wilde have expanded on the evaluation model originally developed by R. H. Orr, as shown in Figure 9.3. This revised model clearly demonstrates the wide variety of measures that can be selected by a library and differentiates the activities in the library are performed by staff to prepare materials for use (Technical Processes) from the activities performed by staff that interact with the users of the library (Public Processes). It is important to remember that a performance measure is simply a quantitative description of what is and the measure requires some context and analysis in order to understand its underlying meaning.

Ultimately the success of a library director and of the library's budget is a political judgment on the part of the various stakeholders, particularly the funding decision makers, and of the citizens themselves (especially if they are called upon to vote for an increased tax levy) about the utility and value of the public library in their community.

A positive judgment is accomplished by first identifying the strategies that the library will be using to deliver the service responses it has selected that will be most responsive to its community. Then the public library should identify that set of input, process, output, and outcome measures that will reflect the contribution of the library to individuals and to the community, as shown in Figure 9.4 (page 166). Once these measures have been selected, it is important to ensure that the collection and use of the measures is clearly understood by all library staff members. To achieve the library's vision of the future, goals are set for each measure (usually interim goals are also established). Finally, the performance measures are collected and distributed to all staff members and stakeholders on a quarterly basis. The measures are then discussed in regular library management and staff meetings so that it becomes clear what they are reflecting. Corrective actions, if any, can then be discussed and planned.

It is also important to select performance measures of activities and services over which the library has complete control. An effective performance measurement system has the following attributes:

- **Clarity of purpose.** The audience for whom the measures are being collected and analyzed is clearly stated. Those in the target audience should readily understand the indicators.

- **Focus.** The measures chosen should reflect the service objectives of the library.

- **Alignment.** The performance measures should be synchronized with the goals and objectives of the library. Too many libraries routinely collect too many statistics and performance measures that then are blithely ignored.

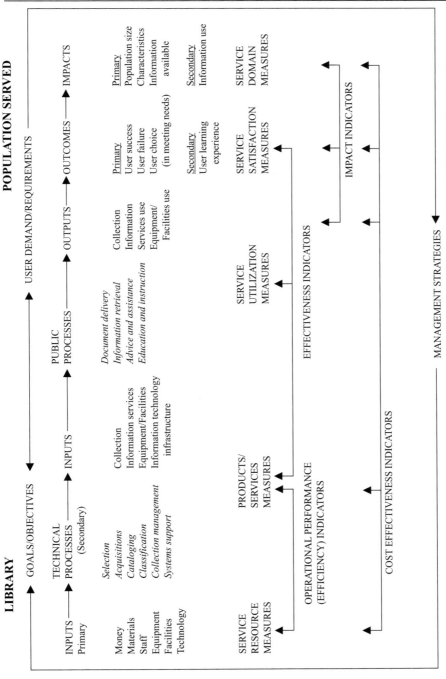

Figure 9.3. Performance Measure Framework. Adapted from Neil McLean and Clare Wilde. Evaluating Library Performance: The Search for Relevance. *Australian Academic & Research Libraries,* 22 (3), September 1991, 201.

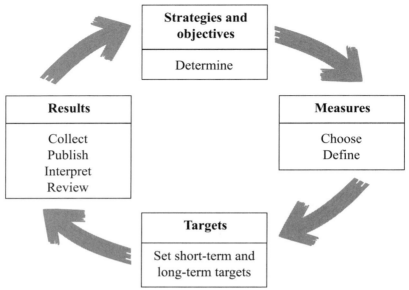

Figure 9.4. Approach to Performance Measurement

- **Balance.** The measures that are selected for use should present a balanced view of the library and its performance. Some of the measures should include outcomes and the user perspective. Measures describe different characteristics of performance:

    - *Absolute/relative.* An absolute measure is one that can stand on its own. A relative performance measure is compared to the same measures in other "similar" libraries.

    - *Process/function oriented.* A process measure looks at the various tasks and activities that comprise a functional activity, for example, cataloging. A functional measure takes a broader view.

    - *Performance or diagnostic.* Some performance measures are designed to measure the achievements of a particular service; others are gathered to assist in analyzing a process or activity with the goal of improving the activity.

    - *Objective/subjective.* Objective measures reflect a specific activity, for example, circulation, whereas a subjective measure reflects an opinion or observation by a trained professional, such as adequacy and depth of a children's collection, or by citizens, through, for example, satisfaction surveys. Sometimes objective data are referred to as "hard measures"; subjective data have been called "soft measures."

- *Direct/indirect.* A direct indicator measures a specific activity (e.g., circulation). An indirect indicator provides an estimate for an activity (the number of online catalog searches to estimate number of people who used the online catalog—e.g., 2.5 searches = 1 person).

- *Leading/lagging.* A leading performance measure provides some advance warning that another activity will increase or decrease. A lagging measure reflects actual performance, such as circulation.

- *Social/economic.* Combinations of social and economic outcome measures are used.

- **Regular refinement.** The performance indicators that are collected should be periodically reviewed to ensure that their continued use provides the library with real value. In some cases, a new measure should be introduced and another should be dropped.

- **Vigorous performance indicators.** Each performance measure should be clearly defined and relevant. The data collected should be unambiguous and not open to manipulation. Readily available statistics, such as the number of Web site hits, are often more dangerous than useful.

The selection, collection, and sharing of performance measures is designed to provide improved services as well as increased accountability by informing all of the library's stakeholders of how well the library is actually doing. Figure 9.5 identifies the wide range of possible performance measures that a public library can choose to use. The library might want to consider grouping the measures into three or four categories, as shown in the figure.

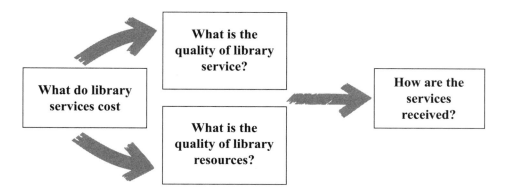

Figure 9.5. Public Library Performance Measures

Among the measures that are reported to stakeholders there should be a balance among input, process (efficiency), output, and outcome measures. Possible performance measures include the following:

- What do library services cost?

    - Library budget expenditures per capita

    - Materials expenditures per capita

    - Proportion of materials expenditures spent on electronic resources

    - Cost of technical services per item added to the collection

    - Cost-benefit analysis or return on investment (ROI)

- What is the quality of library services?

    - Open hours per week

    - Number of public access computers

    - Reliability of the computer network and systems

    - Number of children's programs

    - Social benefits for each service response

    - Economic benefits for each service response

- What is the quality of the collection and access to electronic resources?

    - Immediate availability of collection materials

    - Number of titles/volumes added to the collection

    - Percent of collection added in last five years, ten years

    - Number of full-text periodicals accessible using electronic resources

- How are the services accepted?

    - Market penetration (active users as a percent of total population)

    - Circulation per capita

    - Reference questions per capita

    - User satisfaction survey

> *Managers are not confronted with problems that are independent of each other, but with dynamic situations that consist of complex systems of changing problems that interact with each other. I call such situations messes. . . . Managers do not solve problems: they manage messes.*—Russell Ackoff [17]

These measures are meant to be illustrative rather than prescriptive. It is also important to provide some context to each of these measures so that library stakeholders will know whether a market penetration figure, for example, is better than, about the same as, or less than other comparable libraries. In addition, it might be illuminating to provide information about the set of performance measures over the course of the last four or five years so that people will have a better idea about possible trends. An example of how a library might present this information about a set of performance measures is shown in Figure 9.6 (pages 170–172). This approach relies on presenting the information in graphical form so that trends are immediately apparent.

An alternative presentation of performance measures is shown in Table 9.1 (page 173). This particular arrangement of performance measures reflects the different viewpoints that can be employed for a particular library service. It is important to note that this approach requires the library to articulate in writing an objective that states an improvement for a specific set of users. This approach can be expanded by subdividing the "outcomes" column into three columns: initial, intermediate, and long-term.

The Balanced Scorecard

One approach to communicating value and performance that has taken on an increasingly important role in profit, nonprofit, and governmental agencies is the use of the balanced scorecard. The scorecard approach is based on answering four basic questions, each defining a perspective on the library's value:

- How do customers see the public library?

- What must the library excel at? (internal perspective)

- Can the library continue to improve and create value? (innovation and learning perspective)

- How does the public library look to stakeholders? (financial perspective)

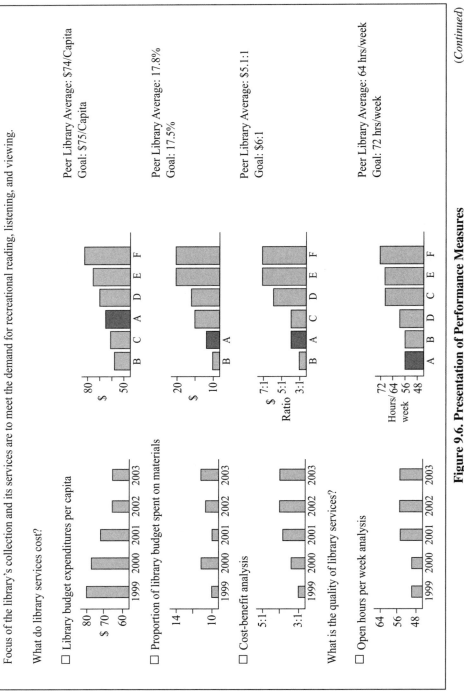

Figure 9.6. Presentation of Performance Measures

(Continued)

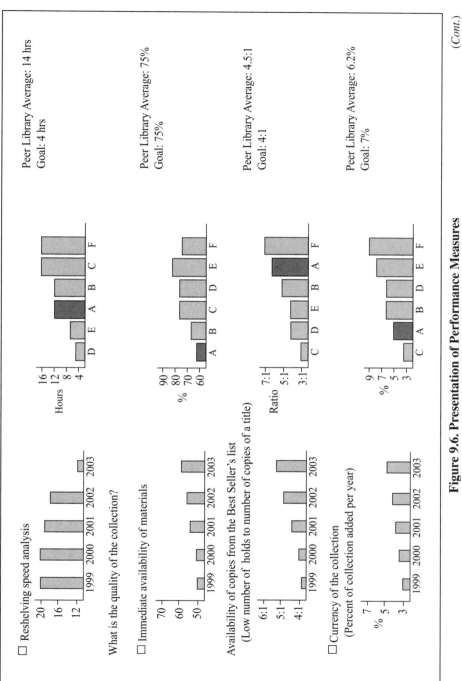

Figure 9.6. Presentation of Performance Measures

(Cont.)

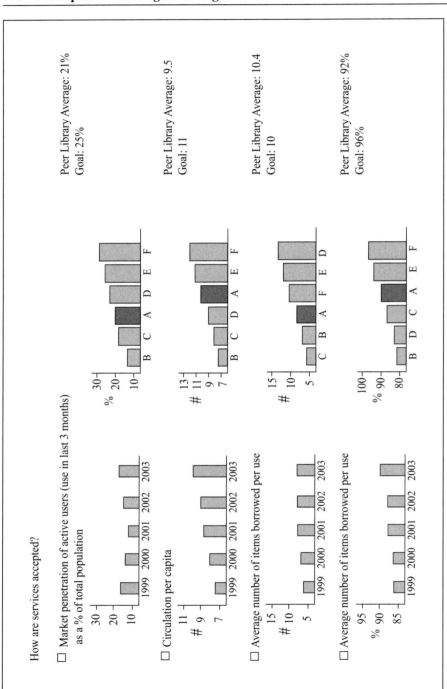

Figure 9.6. Presentation of Performance Measures

(*Cont.*)

Table 9.1. Potential Performance Measures

Service Area	Objective	Input	Output	Efficiency	Service Quality	Outcomes
Lending of popular books, audio and video materials	To increase the percent of the community who borrows popular materials at least a year from X% to Y%	Budget of staff that supports lending of popular materials Materials acquisitions budget Materials acquisitions budget as a % of the total budget	Total number of items loaned per year (Circulation) Circulation per capita Collection turnover rate	Cost per item borrowed Cost to order, receive, and processes materials	Availability rate Number of days to get a copy of a book on the best seller's list	Cost-benefit ratio Customer satisfaction The percent of the community who borrows popular materials at least four times a year
Provide access to electronic full-text journals	To increase the percent of the community who gain access to electronic full-text journals from X% to Y%	Budget for electronic full-text journals Budget for electronic full-text journals as a % of the total budget	Number of individuals who use electronic full-text journals Number of electronic full-text journals titles Number of electronic full-text journals articles downloaded	Cost of electronic full-text journals per title Cost of electronic full-text journals per user Cost of electronic full-text journals per Capita	Time when electronic full-text journals are not accessible (downtime – as a % of 168 hours per week) Responsive time to log on to service Response time to down load a 1MB file with a 56 Kb modem	Cost-benefit ratio Customer satisfaction The percent of the community who gains access to the electronic full-text journals at least 4 times a year
Reference services	To increase the percent of the community who uses reference services at least four times a year from X% to Y%	Budget of reference staff Reference materials acquisitions budget	Number of reference questions answered (directional questions are excluded) Number of individuals who attend an information literacy class	Cost of reference services per question answered Cost of reference services per capita	Accuracy of reference answers Completeness of reference answers	Customer satisfaction The percent of the community who uses the reference service at least 4 times a year
Children's services	To increase the percent of the community who uses the children's services at least four times a year from X% to Y%	Budget of children's services staff Children's materials acquisitions budget Children's materials acquisitions budget as a percent of the total materials acquisitions budget	Circulation of children's materials Circulation of children's materials per capita Children's materials turnover rate Attendance at children's activities—story hours	Cost per item borrowed Cost to order, receive, and process materials Cost of children's services staff per capita Cost of children's services staff per story hour attendee	Availability rate Number of days to get a copy of a children's book on the hold (request) list	Cost-benefit ratio Customer satisfaction The percent of the community who borrows children's materials at least four times a year The percent of the community who attends children's activities at least four times a year

Providing a set of performance measures for each perspective simultaneously lets one see "whether improvements in one area may have been achieved at the expense of another." Using this approach means that the library can consider disparate elements of the competitive agenda such as becoming more customer oriented, shortening response times, improving collection quality, emphasizing teamwork, or developing new services altogether.

Viewing a variety of performance indicators that are focused on the four perspectives allows management to take a broader view. The library does not just pursue circulation, or customer satisfaction, or expenditures on fiction, in isolation. Rather, the scorecard provides a vehicle that allows the management team and library staff members to see how their combined actions are reflected in the performance indicators considered as a uniform set.[18] An overview of the balanced scorecard is presented in Figure 9.7.

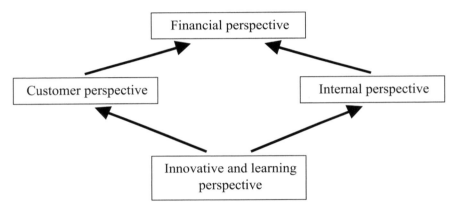

Figure 9.7. The Balanced Scorecard

The idea behind the scorecard is to formulate targets in each of the four areas (three to five measures in each) and to select interim goals for each target:

- *Customer perspective (users):* Customer concerns tend to fall into four categories: time, quality, performance and service, and cost. A variety of customer-focused measures can be employed, including customer satisfaction (although customer satisfaction surveys must be used cautiously in a library setting due to their positively skewed results).

- *Internal perspective:* Managers should focus on these critical internal operations that enable them to satisfy customer needs. This part of the scorecard looks at the processes and competencies a public library must excel at. In addition to productivity measures, technological capability, introduction of new ideas, and monitoring/evaluation mechanisms might be addressed.

- *Innovation and learning perspective:* This looks at the library's ability to grow, learn, develop, and introduce new services. It focuses on measures such as introduction of new services, infrastructure, and the skills of library staff members.

- *Financial perspective:* In the nonprofit, governmental arena of a public library, financial measures such as profitability are not relevant. But the library can, and must, demonstrate that it makes effective use of the funding that is provided.

The assumption is that the innovative perspective (dealing with infrastructure and the quality of staff) will create a more efficient operation (internal perspective). The combination of staff, infrastructure, and internal operations will lead to products and services that will be more appealing to customers. The customers are then going to purchase more products and services, leading to better financial results (financial perspective).

Since traditional measurement systems sprang from the finance function, the performance measurement systems have a control bias. That is, traditional performance measurement systems specify the particular actions they want employees to take and then measure to see whether the employees have in fact taken those actions. In that way, the systems try to control behavior.

The balanced scorecard, on the other hand, puts strategy and vision, not control, at the center. It establishes goals but assumes that people will adopt whatever behavior and take whatever actions are necessary to help achieve those goals. The goal is to minimize the gap that exists between the mission and performance measures. The focus should be on what the library intends to achieve, not the programs and initiatives that are being implemented.

The balanced scorecard provides a useful framework that serves as the focal point when a library is trying to draw up performance measures for the library. The system is based on the understanding that no *single* measure can focus attention on all of the critical areas of the service. And the set of performance measures that are selected must work together coherently to achieve the overall goals of the library.

Robert Kaplan has suggested an alternative scorecard for nonprofit organizations, as shown in Figure 9.8 (page 176).

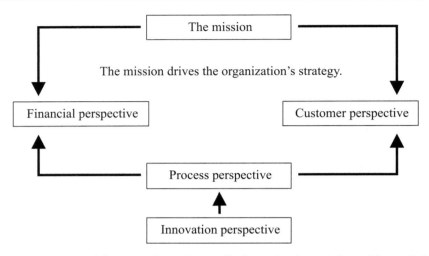

Figure 9.8. Balanced Scorecard for Nonprofit Organizations. Adapted from Robert S. Kaplan. Strategic Performance Measurement and Management in Nonprofit Organizations. *Nonprofit Management & Leadership***, 11 (3), Spring 2001, 353–70.**

A Library Scorecard

Rather than using the original balanced scorecard with its four perspectives that were created for for-profit firms, a revised balanced scorecard may be more appropriate for public libraries, which exist in the governmental arena. In addition to a reorganized structure, the library balanced scorecard introduces an additional perspective: *information resources* (see Figure 9.9). These information resources comprise the library's physical collection, the access to electronic databases subscribed to by the library, and resources obtained from other sources, such as through interlibrary loan or a document delivery service.

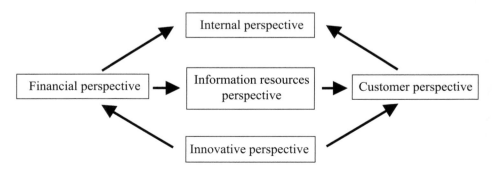

Figure 9.9. The Library Scorecard

The library scorecard model suggests that the financial resources provided to the library are used to provide the information resources, staff (which uses a variety of processes and procedures measured using the internal perspective), and infrastructure, as well as providing staff training. All of these are combined to provide services to users (the customer perspective).

Public libraries with branches might also want to consider using one or more performance measures that communicate the adequacy, age, size, and condition of each branch library as well as a composite index for all library facilities (perhaps add a facilities perspective). Such measures might help the library's funding decision makers and other stakeholders understand the need to plan for building new branch library facilities or to remodel existing facilities.

In addition to recognizing that several perspectives should be used to demonstrate the value and contributions of the public library, a combination of different types of performance measures are likely to be needed, as shown in Table 9.1 (page 173).

In addition, depending upon the interests of the library and its various stakeholders, such as, organizational health, efficiency, quality and effectiveness, a different combination of measures may be needed, as shown in Table 9.2 (page 178).

Table 9.2. Performance Measurement Grid

Attributes	Input Measures	Process Measures	Output Measures	Outcomes or Impacts
Organizational health	Competitive salary and benefits Staff training hours		Staff morale Staff turnover	Reputation of staff: friendly or helpful or . . .
Efficiency	Budget Staff Collections Facilities Technology	Unit costs Time to complete Staff productivity Information system activity	Within budget Services used Use of collections/ Building activity Catalog/portal use	
Quality		Number of errors Best practice compared to others	Completeness and accuracy LibQUAL+	Minimal corrections
Effectiveness			Customer satisfaction Best use of resources	Adds value to community Social benefits Economic benefits for the individual Economic benefits for the community Meets demand: priority and performance evaluation Results endure Recognition and acclaim

The Library Index

An alternative perspective is being developed by a group of German public libraries involved in a project to build The Library Index. The approach being taken is a variation of a balanced scorecard that combines 15 performance indicators into a single library index.[19] These 15 indicators are grouped into four categories or perspectives, as shown in Table 9.3. Note that all of these measures are either input or output measures and that no attempts have been made to use outcome or impact measures.

Table 9.3. Library Index Performance Indicators

Mission Fulfillment (Quantity)	Customer Focus (Quality)
Collection size/population	Number of visits
Total square feet/1,000 population	Circulation/population
Staff/1,000 population	Collection turnover rate
Renewals (percent of circulation)	Hours open
Financial	**Staff Orientation**
Collection budget/circulation	Absenteeism rate
Number of staff hours/open hours	Further education rate
Visits/square foot	Fluctuation rate (3-year average)
Total budget/visit (gate count)	

Keys to Success

A manual developed by King Research provided a standardized approach to performance measurement for British public libraries. This manual proscribed a number of performance measures and indicators and defined a performance measure as something that described in quantitative terms, such as annual circulation. A performance indicator, expressed quantitatively, implies something about the performance of the organization or some aspect of its operations.[20] The performance measures were grouped into four categories, as shown in Table 9.4 (page 180).

Table 9.4. King Research Performance Measure Categories

Service input cost measures

PM 1	Amount of resources applied to each service (financial, staff, facilities, equipment and systems, collections, other)
PM 2	Amount of funding applied to each service (all resources converted into monetary terms)
PM 3	Attributes of the service that affect the cost and/or the quantity and/or quality of outputs (for example, size of geographic area and number of branch libraries)

Service output measures

PM 4	Quantities of output for each service
PM 5	Quality of output based on a 1 to 5 scale of grade or goodness.
PM 6	Timeliness of output or the time between a request being made and the material to satisfy the request being received by the user
PM 7	Availability of service (the number of hours the service is available)
PM 8	Accessibility of the service (time a user must travel to reach the library)

Service effectiveness measures

PM 9	Amount of use (loans, visits, use of reference, photocopiers, events, story hours, and so forth)
PM 10	Users' perceptions of attributes (rate general service performance or an attribute of service on a 1 to 5 scale)
PM 11	User-expressed satisfaction on a 1 to 5 scale
PM 12	User-indicated importance (priority) on a 1 to 5 scale
PM 13	Purpose of use (categorize users' purposes, e.g., educational, recreational, work-related, and so forth)
PM 14	Consequences of use (while all purposes of use have some implications in terms of quality of life, the economy and other higher-order effects, the manual did not provide any suggestions on how to measure these effects)

Service domain measures

PM 15	Total size of population
PM 16	Population attributes, categorizing population by location of residence, age, gender, occupation, and so on
PM 17	User population size (count of registered borrowers, number of visitors to the library)
PM 18	User population attributes (categorizing user population by location of residence, age, gender, occupation, and so on)
PM 19	Size of service geographic area
PM 20	Geographic area attributes (population density, availability of public transportation)
PM 21	Information needs (by type of need or type of material needed)

Adapted from King Research. *Keys to Success: Performance Indicators for Public Libraries*. Library Information Series No. 18. London: HMSO, 1990. See also Peter Brophy and Kate Coulling. *Quality Management for Information and Library Managers*. London: Aslib-Gower, 1996.

The specified performance indicators include those shown in Table 9.5.

Table 9.5. King Research Performance Indicators

Operational performance indicators (relate input to output)

PI 1	Productivity, calculated by dividing the number of outputs by input costs (number of reference queries per hour of staff time)
PI 2	Cost per output (cost per reference query)
PI 3	Cost by attribute level—to provide information on the relationship between attributes and costs (for example, the average cost per output may increase as staff spend more time to improve the accuracy of a reference query)
PI 4	Productivity by attribute levels (number of items cataloged per hour of staff time)

Effectiveness indicators (relate output to use)

PI 5	Turnover rate—the relationship between the amount provided and the amount used (use of the collection, categorized by the age of the collection)
PI 6	Amount of use by attribute level (indicates how attributes of output [timeliness, accessibility, and so forth] influence the amount of use of a service)
PI 7	User satisfaction (divided into general satisfaction, satisfaction with specific services, or attributes of a service)
PI 8	User satisfaction by attribute level (how user satisfaction varies with different attribute levels)
PI 9	Amount of use by satisfaction level (amount of use of children's services divided by the level of user satisfaction with those levels)

Cost-effectiveness indicators (relate input to use)

PI 10	Cost per use—total input costs divided by the amount of use
PI 11	Cost per user (input costs divided by the number of actual users of a service)
PI 12	Cost per capita
PI 13	Cost by satisfaction level (higher satisfaction levels may require higher input costs)

Impact indicators (relate use to potential use)

PI 14	Users as a proportion of the population (overall and for specific services)
PI 15	User per capita (overall and for specific services)
PI 16	Needs fill rate (proportion of identified needs that are actually met).

Adapted from *King Research. Keys to Success: Performance Indicators for Public Libraries. Library Information Series No. 18.* London: HMSO, 1990. See also Peter Brophy and Kate Coulling. *Quality Management for Information and Library Managers.* London: Aslib-Gower, 1996.

Even a quick glance at the these performance measures and indicators from *Keys to Success* will reveal that the majority of the measures and indicators are input and process oriented, and other than satisfaction, no attempt is made to identify the outcomes of the public library on the community.

Summary

The importance of demonstrating the value of the public library to its various stakeholders has become clearer in recent years. Performance measures have become more sophisticated as various researchers and librarians have attempted to develop tools and methodologies that will help the practicing librarian demonstrate value.

Developing a culture of assessment is fundamental for librarians to have a better understanding of the needs of the communities that they serve as well as understanding how their actions have an impact on their users. Ultimately the ability of the public librarian to convince funding decision makers of the value and utility of the library is evidenced by the library's ability to acquire the necessary resources to maintain and expand the services of the public library.

It is also important to remember that a set of performance measures that are used by one library may not be applicable in another setting. Too often, public libraries focus on "measuring the measurable" rather than selecting a set of measures that will reveal the success of the strategies employed by the library to deliver its services. Finally, the performance measures are only surrogates of the service itself. The purpose of the measures is to allow the library staff and stakeholders to begin a discussion of the role of the library in the community and how successful the library is in meeting the needs of its users.

Notes

1. Quoted by Jan Hunt at www.naturalchild.com/jan_hunt/grading.html (accessed August 5, 2003).

2. Peter Hernon and Ellen Altman. *Assessing Service Quality: Satisfying the Expectations of Library Customers*. Chicago: American Library Association, 1998, 55.

3. Barry Totterdell and Jean Bird. *The Effective Library: Report of the Hillingdon Project on Public Library Effectiveness*. London: The Library Association, 1976.

4. Ibid.

5. Michael K. Buckland. *Library Services in Theory and Context*. New York: Pergamon Press, 1988.

6. Jennifer Cram. Performance Management, Measurement and Reporting in a Time of Information-Centred Change. *The Australian Library Journal*, 45 (3), August 1996, 225–38.

7. Larry Nash White. Does Counting Count: An Evaluative Study of the Use and Impact of Performance Measurement in Florida Public Libraries. Ph.D. Dissertation, Florida State University, Tallahassee, 2002.

8. Peter F. Drucker. *Managing in the Next Society*. New York: St. Martin's Press, 2002, 79.

9. Susan B. Barnard. Implementing Total Quality Management: A Model for Research Libraries. *Journal of Academic Librarianship*, 18, 1993, 57–70.

10. Amos Lakos. Library Management Information Systems in the Client Server Environment: A Proposed New Model. *Proceedings of the 2nd Northumbria International Conference on Performance Measurement & Libraries & Information Services*. New Castle, England: University of Northumbria, 1998, 277–86.

11. Ibid.

12. Thomas J. Peters and Robert H. Waterman Jr. *In Search of Excellence: Lessons from America's Best-Run Companies*. New York: Harper & Row, 1982.

13. Howard M. Armitage and Vijay M. Jog. Creating & Measuring Shareholder Value: A Canadian Perspective. *Ivey Business Journal*, 63 (5), July/August 1999, 75–81.

14. Lord Kelvin. *Popular Lectures & Addresses, 1891–1894.* Cited in *Bartlett's Familiar Quotations,* 16th ed., Justin Kaplan, general ed. Boston: Little, Brown, 1992, 504.

15. Jacob Viner. *Essays on the Intellectual History of Economics*, Douglas A. Irwin (Ed.). Princeton, NJ: Princeton University Press, 1991.

16. Cram. Performance Management.

17. Quoted in Donald A. Schon. *The Reflective Practitioner: How Professionals Think in Action*. New York: Basic Books, 1983, 16.

18. Charles Birch. *Future Success: A Balanced Approach to Measuring and Improving Success in Your Organization.* New York: Prentice-Hall, 2000; Mark Graham Brown. *Winning Score: How to Design and Implement Organizational Scorecards.* Portland, OR: Productivity, 2000; Robert S. Kaplan and David P. Norton. *The Strategy-Focused Organization: How Balanced Scorecard Companies Thrive in the New Business Environment.* Boston: Harvard Business School Press, 2001; Robert S. Kaplan and David P. Norton. *The Balanced Scorecard: Translating Strategy into Action.* Boston: Harvard Business School Press, 1996.

19. Petra Klug. BIX—The Library Index, or: Why Less Is Often More. *Performance Measurement and Metrics*, 1(2), August 2000, 129–34.

20.	King Research. *Keys to Success: Performance Indicators for Public Libraries*. Library Information Series No. 18. London: HMSO, 1990. See also Peter Brophy and Kate Coulling. *Quality Management for Information and Library Managers*. London: Aslib-Gower, 1996.

Communicating Value

The field is not well seen from within the field.—Ralph Waldo Emerson[1]

Public libraries have historically done little in the way of creating a proactive communication program to inform their various stakeholders and customers of the value of the library. Historically, librarians have selected a range of performance measures, consisting primarily of input and output measures, to communicate value. Unfortunately, what is important to librarians may not necessarily be important to various stakeholders, including funding decision makers. Therefore, it is important to focus on the information needs of stakeholders. Using a set of performance measures, once you have the information about the impact of your library on the individual and community, "spotlight the message!" Communicate a consistent message, using conventional and unusual methods, that library services are valuable to the community.

Effectively communicating the benefits of public library services is as important as managing a well-run library and identifying what performance measures to use. Developing a communications strategy or plan identifies the several ways the value of the public library will be communicated to a variety of stakeholders. From the perspective of the stakeholder, being presented with numerous facts and figures still doesn't communicate the impact that the public library has on individuals and on the community itself. In putting together this communications strategy, it is important to remember several concerns, discussed below.

A profession that sees itself as "doing good" is less concerned with assessing its outcomes and impacts since it sees its own activities as inherently positive.—Amos Lakos[2]

185

Glen Holt has suggested that a consistent multimedia public relations campaign has several benefits, including to[3]

- Increase use of the library,

- Encourage library users to use additional library services,

- Inform nonusers about library services and how they fit into their busy lives, and

- Inform the general population about the value of the local public library.

Understand Your Audience

One of the primary reasons that information about the value of the library is not well received or understood is that the information being presented does not acknowledge the audience's perspective. The funding decision makers for the local public library, be they a city manager, the mayor, city council members, members of the board of supervisors, a library board, or other key individuals, are the principal audience for the message concerning the value of the public library. These individuals want to know that the library uses the financial resources in a responsible and cost-efficient manner and that the community values and appreciates the services available at the local library.

A national survey of library directors and public officials demonstrated a wide gap in perception when comparing the value of the public library to other community services (police, fire, streets, and parks and recreation).[4] Although three-fourths of the library directors felt that they initiated interactions with local public officials, only slightly more than one-half of the local officials agreed. There was, however, general agreement about the extent to which library and public officials perceived that they agree with each other on the goals, importance, and quality of the public library.

Try to develop relationships with the funding decision makers so that you understand how they prefer to receive information. Some people are auditory learners, some visual (graphic) learners, and still others prefer to read textual material. Visit with them on their turf and learn what their current problems and priorities are to determine whether the library can provide information that will be of value to them.

> *Never impose your language on people you wish to reach.*—Abbie Hoffman[5]

The choice of performance measures that reflect the benefits of public library services is obviously important. The selection of these measures must be made with the understanding that the resulting information has to be relevant to local decision makers. In addition, the information being communicated to these stakeholders must be understandable to the nonlibrarian. Clearly the information being communicated must be free of library jargon and acronyms. For example, "circulation per capita" will mean little to most stakeholders. However, "the number of items borrowed per capita" or "the number of checkouts per capita" will have more meaning to the funding decision makers.

Provide Context

Raw statistical data will have little meaning to those the library is trying to impress. Providing some context or comparison about what a particular statistic means will significantly improve the communication process. Mentioning that "circulation per capita" is among the highest 10 percent in the state for comparable libraries will have greater meaning than the number itself. Comparing the weekly or monthly attendance at the public library to attendance at sporting events or the local movie theater may provide a more meaningful impression about how frequently the library is used. Develop zippy one-liners such as "public library services for 'x' cents per day per citizen," or "we provide library services for 'y' cents per use" or "the entire population of 'your city' visits the library every 'z' days!"

In some cases, especially for larger public libraries, providing the statistical information in map format has real appeal since this is something that local stakeholders see on a fairly frequent basis. It is relatively easy to import data into a geographical information system (GIS) and then produce some fairly striking maps revealing library use across the jurisdiction.

Perceptions of the Public Library

Statements that describe public libraries and their services resonate well with the general public, according to a 2002 survey conducted on behalf of the American Library Association.[6] The statements in support of libraries that were either "very convincing" or "somewhat convincing" include the following:

Libraries are changing and dynamic places	91%
Libraries are places of opportunity	90%
Libraries are unique	88%
Libraries are a place of lifelong learning	88%
Libraries are your neighborhood's "How To" resource	88%
Librarians are information navigators	86%
Libraries bring you the world	85%
Librarians are the ultimate search engine	84%
Free people need free libraries	83%
Librarians are techno-savvy	81%

Be Credible

The factors that influence your credibility are expertise and trustworthiness. A library director who is active in the community will build trust and will be better received when making presentations about the library and its value. Work to determine how the public library can provide services to the government management team.

When presenting information about the use of a particular set of performance measures, it is important to

- ensure that the results of any survey that has been conducted are accurate and that the survey did not have any methodology problems (e.g., concerns about sample size, sample bias, and so forth);

- document the process for how the data for each measure were collected;

- compare your results with the results of other comparable libraries in your state or nationally; and

- contrast your results with those noted in the literature.

Improve Presentation Skills

Effective communication occurs when the choice of medium being used to communicate the message is appropriate for the size of the group, as shown in Figure 10.1. Having a clear goal of the message or messages that the library wants to communicate is the foundation upon which all communication about the value of the public library rests.

Presenting information in graphic form can be a much more effective way to communicate the library's message. However, care must be exercised in the use of graphics, as the availability of such programs as PowerPoint has made such graphical presentations too routine and humdrum. Some suggestions for improving the use of graphical presentations follow:

- Make the number of graphics quite small.

- Make sure the graphic can stand on its own and minimize text.

- A simple (and memorable) graphic is preferred over the complex.

- Test each graphic. Make sure it is communicating the message you intend.[7]

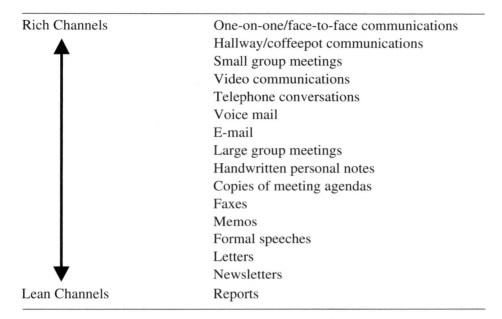

Rich Channels	One-on-one/face-to-face communications
	Hallway/coffeepot communications
	Small group meetings
	Video communications
	Telephone conversations
	Voice mail
	E-mail
	Large group meetings
	Handwritten personal notes
	Copies of meeting agendas
	Faxes
	Memos
	Formal speeches
	Letters
	Newsletters
Lean Channels	Reports

Figure 10.1. Communication Continuum. Adapted from Joseph M. Miniace and Elizabeth Falter. Communication: A Key Factor in Strategy Implementation. *Planning Review*, **January–February 1996, 29.**

Stage the Release of Information

The process of communicating the value of the local library is something that should occur all during the course of the year rather than simply when releasing the library's annual report. A combination of written and oral messages should be conveyed using press releases and formal and informal presentations before civic organizations, interested groups, and the funding stakeholders.

The library can produce a range of written materials to more effectively communicate the message that the public library provides real value to the community:

- Look for creative ways to use a human-interest perspective to make the contributions of the public library come alive in newspaper articles.

- Prepare an executive summary of the library's annual report (two pages) that is well designed and has real visual appeal (consider using colorful graphics, charts, and so forth).

- Use the library's monthly newsletter to focus on the progress being made to achieve the goals of the library.

- Use bookmarks as a way to get your message out.

- Prepare an article to submit to one of the professional library journals documenting your experiences and results.

The librarian can prepare formal presentations (using PowerPoint slides and handouts) as well as be prepared to give informal, brief talks to small-group meetings. The hallmark of a good salesperson is to prepare a succinct "elevator speech" that provides a summary of the message. The library director and management team members should practice their elevator speeches about the value of the library.

Storytelling puts information in context and is a way to make facts and figures come alive. Stories are how we make sense of things. Consistently collect and use "war stories." A good story is often the best way to convey the message about the value of the library and its information services. Stories have a human voice and help us to communicate in a way that will help the listener remember the message better. Begin your next presentation by saying, "Let me tell you a story . . ."

Ask for Feedback

Ask a variety of stakeholders for a review and critique of the library's communication strategy and your particular presentations skills. Different people have different ways in which they prefer to receive and absorb information: visual, through a conversation, listening to a formal presentation, reading a brief synopsis, and so forth. Taking to heart the candid comments of stakeholders will give you the opportunity to improve your presentation skills and fine-tune your message regarding the value of the public library so that it will resonate with your local stakeholders.

Whatever measures are chosen by the library, it is important to show trends over time just as corporations do in their annual reports. Showing data for the last five years will typically provide enough perspective to demonstrate any trends.

Summary

As the library director and members of the library's management team communicate with stakeholders, staff members, and customers, remember that:

- Politics is at least as important as measuring library outcomes.

- You should cultivate your library's stakeholders, even when you don't need anything.

- Don't oversell your library services—*over-deliver.*[8] Look for ways to personalize the library services experienced by your customers—whether in person or online.[9]

- Convey the message of the value of the public library vividly but succinctly. Convert the library's annual budget to a cost per day per capita. Identity the number of days it takes for the entire population of the community to visit the public library (total population divided by daily gate count times "x" number of days).

- Talk to public library stakeholders one on one whenever possible.

- Rather than using dry statistics, provide some context for your information that will be understandable in the environment within which the library operates. For example, convert the annual number of people visiting the library (in person and online) to the number of times a nearby football stadium would be filled up.

- Present information in terms that the audience will understand. Translate numbers, be they dollars or statistics, into terms that have a real associative meaning so that the bottom line message of the library will be heard, understood, and remembered.

- Communicating the value of the library is "job number 1" for the public library director. Make sure you devote the time and energy needed to always be prepared to deliver your library's message.

Notes

1. *Essays and English Traits,* IX; *Circles,* 1841. *The Harvard Classics, 1909–14.* Available at www.bartleby.com/5/109.html (accessed August 5, 2003).

2. Amos Lakos. The Missing Ingredient—Culture of Assessment in Libraries. *Performance Measurement and Metrics,* Sample Issue, August 1999, 3–7.

3. Glen E. Holt. Balancing Buildings, Books, Bytes, and Bucks: Steps to Secure the Public Library future in the Internet Age. *Library Trends,* 46 (1), Summer 1997, 92–116.

4. The Library Research Center. A Survey of Public Libraries and Local Government. *Illinois State Library Special Report Series,* 4 (1), 1997, 1–62.

5. Abbie Hoffman. *Revolution for the Hell of It.* New York: Dial Press, 1968.

6. KRC Research & Consulting. *@ Your Library: Attitudes Toward Public Libraries survey.* June 2002. Available at: http://www.ala.org/pio/presskits/nlw2002kit/krc_data.pdf (accessed June 16, 2003).

7. Richard Saul Wurman. *Information Anxiety 2*. Indianapolis, IN: Que, 2001.

8. Tom Peters. *Thriving on Chaos*. New York: Pan Books, 1989.

9. Kevin Davis. The Changing Role of the Business Librarian. *Knowledge Management*, December 1998. Available at: http://enterprise.supersites.net/knmagn2/km199812/fc1.htm (accessed June 16, 2003).

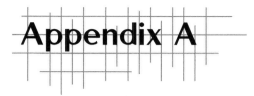

Appendix A

Input Measures, Process Measures, Outcome Measures, and Satisfaction-Based Outcome Measures

Input Measures

Measure	Definition
Clients (Users)	
Number of professionals in the organization	Count of the number of professionals in the organization. For example, lawyers, doctors, researchers, consultants, and so forth.
Total registered clients	Count of the number of registered clients (those who have been issued a library card)
Registered clients per capita	Count of the number of registered clients divided by the total population More accurately, the library should measure number of registered residents in a government jurisdiction compared to total population in the jurisdiction.
Registered nonresidents	Count of the number of registered clients who live outside the service boundaries (for example, city boundaries)
Registered nonresidents per capita	Count of the number of registered nonresidents divided by the total population
Total active registered users (used the library in the last year)	Count of the number of registered users who have used the library in the last year. Uses include borrowing of materials, use of reference services, browsing the collection and so forth

Measure	Definition
Population of legal service area	Count of the potential population to be served
Percent of population living within a certain distance of a library	Count of the population living within a certain distance of a library divided by the total population
Demographics of clients (sorted by residents and non-residents)	Statistical information about the registered clients (sorted by residents and nonresidents)
Budget	
Total budget of the library	Total budget allocation, in dollars
Budget expenditures per professional staff member in the organization	Total budget allocation divided by the number of professional staff members in the larger organization
Budget expenditures for acquisitions	Proportion of budget spent on acquiring materials for the library's collection, expressed as a percentage
Materials acquisitions budget as a percent of the total budget	Proportion of budget spent on acquiring materials for the library's collection, expressed as a percentage
Acquisitions expenditure per item added	Expenditures spent on acquiring materials for the library's collection annually divided by the number of items added to the collection annually
Materials acquisitions budget per capita	Total budget allocation for materials divided by the total potential population served
Budget expenditures for periodicals	Proportion of budget spent on periodical (both print and electronic) subscriptions
Budget expenditures for periodicals per capita	Annual expenditure for periodicals divided by the total population served
Budget expenditures on one category as a proportion of library expenditures spent on all materials	Proportion of budget spent on one category as a proportion of library expenditures spent on all materials, expressed as a percentage

Measure	Definition
Budget expenditures per capita (total potential population served)	Total budget allocation divided by the total potential population served
Acquisitions budget expenditures per capita	Total acquisitions budget divided by the total potential population served
Budget expenditures per FTE library staff	Total budget allocation divided by the total library staff (FTE)
Percent of library materials less than five years old	Number of titles (volumes) purchased in the last five years divided by the total number of titles (volumes)
Expenditure per item added	Budget spent on acquiring materials for the library's collection divided by the total number of items added
Expenditure on staff	Budget spent on paying library staff, usually expressed as a percent of the total library budget
Expenditure per loan	Total budget allocation divided by the total circulation
Capital expenditures	Budget amount devoted to capital expenditures
Local income	Amount of the budget derived from local sources
State income	Amount of the budget derived from state sources
Federal income	Amount of the budget derived from federal sources
Telecommunications expenditures	Budget amount devoted to telecommunications
Computer expenditures	Budget amount devoted to computer-related expenditures

Measure	Definition
Staff	
Number of professional librarians	Total number of librarians (full-time equivalent)
Number of paraprofessionals	Total number of paraprofessionals (full-time equivalent)
Total number of staff	Total number of staff, all classifications (full-time equivalent)
Number of clients served per librarian	Count of the number of clients served divided by the number of librarians (FTE)
Number of clients served per staff member	Count of the number of clients served divided by the number of staff members (FTE)
Population served per staff member	Total population served divided by the total number of staff (FTE)
Number of staff per capita	Count of the total number of staff divided by the total population
Collection	
Total number of titles owned	Count of the total number of titles in the collection
Total number of volumes owned	Count of the total number of volumes in the collection
Total number of volumes checked out	Count of the total number of volumes on loan
Volumes (items) on shelves per capita	Count of the total number of volumes in the collection divided by total population, expressed as XX volumes per person
Total number of volumes (items) on the shelves per capita	Count of the total number of volumes checked out divided by total population, expressed as XX volumes per person
Percent of volumes (items) on loan	Count of the total number of volumes checked out divided by the total number of volumes owned by the library, expressed as XX volumes per person

Measure	Definition
Age of print collection, by five-year increments	Proportion of the print collection based on date of publication sorted in five-year increments
Number of print journal sub-scriptions	Count of the total number of print jour-nal subscriptions
Number of print journal sub-scriptions per capita	Count of the total number of print jour-nal subscriptions divided by the total population served
Number of electronic journal subscriptions	Count of the total number of electronic journal subscriptions
Number of electronic journal subscriptions per capita	Count of the total number of print elec-tronic subscriptions divided by the total population served
Total number of serial titles offered	Count of paper-based journal titles plus count of full-text electronic journals available
Total number of titles pur-chased	Count of the total number of titles added to the collection annually
Total number of volumes purchased	Count of the total number of volumes added to the collection annually
Total number of titles in the collection per capita	Count of the total number of titles in the collection divided by the population served
Total number of audiovisual materials in the collection	Count of the total number of audio-vi-sual items in the collection
Total number of audiovisual materials per capita	Count of the total number of audio-vi-sual items divided by the population served
Age of audiovisual collection, by five-year increments	Proportion of the audiovisual collection based on date of publication sorted in five-year increments
Percent growth of collection	Count of the total number of titles (vol-umes) added to the collection annually divided by the total number of titles (volumes) in the collection at the start of the year, expressed as a percentage

Measure	Definition
Collection exchanges	Count of the total number of titles exchanged with another library/vendor during the year
Titles on order	Count of the total number of titles ordered annually
Titles (volumes) added per year per capita	Count of the total number of titles ordered annually divided by the total population
Feet (meters) of shelving per capita	Linear count, in feet, of available shelving for the collection
Internet Workstations	
Number of public access Internet workstations	Count of the number of library owned public access, Web browser-based workstations that connect to the Internet
Number of public access Internet workstations per capita	Count of the number of library owned public access, Web browser-based workstations that connect to the Internet compared to the service area population, for example, one Internet workstation for every 1,000 service population
Speed of Internet workstations	Effective maximum bandwidth of Internet access—dependent upon the speed of the Internet connection and the speed of the LAN within the library, for example, 56 Kbps, 1.5 Mbps, and so forth
Databases	
Number of online, full-text titles available by subscription	Count of the number of full-text titles available online by subscription
Space	
Total library floor space	Total floor space expressed in square feet

Measure	Definition
Public services floor space	Total floor space dedicated for public use, expressed in square feet
Library area per capita	Total floor space divided by the total population, expressed in XX square feet per person
Number of seats in the library	Count of the number of seats (chairs) for clients to use in the library
Number of seats per capita	Total population divided by the count of the number of seats in the library
Number of service points	Count of the number of service points, for example, circulation desk, reference desk, information desk and so forth.
Availability of library: total hours open per week	Count of the total hours open per week (include hours for the main library plus branch libraries)
Hours open per 100 population	Count of the total hours open annually divided by the total population (in hundreds)
Percent of open hours that fall outside of normal business hours	Number of open hours that fall outside of normal business hours divided by the total number of open hours
Accessibility of library	Average distance or time necessary to travel to the library by users
	Can also be a measure of the physical access features of the library including access for disabled, parking, and so forth.
Equipment per capita	Count of the number of pieces of equipment per capita (and by type)
Number of computer workstations available	Count of the number of computer workstations available for use by clients
Number of computer workstations available per capita	Count of the number of computer workstations available divided by the total population, expressed as a percentage
Computer workstations available annually per capita	Count of the number of computer workstations available times the number of hours the library is open annually divided by the total population, expressed as a percentage

Measure	Definition
Programs for preschool children	Count of the number of programs offered annually for preschool-age children
Programs for school-age children	Count of the number of programs offered annually for school-age children
Total programs for children	Count of the number of programs offered annually for preschool and school-age children
Attendance at preschool programs	Count of the number of children attending preschool programs annually
Attendance at school-age programs	Count of the number of children attending school-age programs annually
Total attendance at children's programs	Count of the number of children attending preschool and school-age programs annually

Process Measures

Measure	Definition
Efficiency	
Cost of acquiring materials	Cost of the material plus staff salaries plus overhead (fringe benefits) to acquire materials for the collection
Cost of cataloging materials	Staff salaries plus overhead (fringe benefits) to catalog materials for the collection (may be broken up into copy cataloging costs, original cataloging costs, and total cataloging costs)
Cost of processing materials	Cost of supplies plus staff salaries plus overhead (fringe benefits) to physically process materials for the collection
Cost of reference services	Staff salaries plus overhead (fringe benefits) to provide reference services
Cost of circulation services	Staff salaries plus overhead (fringe benefits) to provide circulation services

Measure	Definition
Staff Productivity	
Speed of acquiring materials	Elapsed time, in days, from the time an order is placed until the materials are received by the library
Speed of cataloging materials	Elapsed time, in days, from the time materials are received by the library until the cataloging is complete
Speed of processing materials	Elapsed time, in days, from the time materials have their cataloging completed and the materials are placed on the shelf
Speed of reshelving borrowed materials	Elapsed time, in days, from the time materials are returned from circulation until they are returned to the shelves
Time to full materials on hold	Elapsed time, in days, from the time materials are placed on hold until the user is able to check out the item
Library Information System Activity	
System reliability	Total number of hours system is available for use divided by total number of hours system should have been operating, normally expressed as a percentage
System down time (complimentary statistic for System Reliability)	100 percent minus system reliability
Availability of public computer workstations	Number of hours the public computer workstations are available for use divided by the total number of hours the library is open, expressed as a percentage
Facilities	
Average cost per service hour	Total library budget divided by total number of annual open hours
Average number of visitors per service hour	Total number of visitors (gate count) divided by total number of annual open hours

Output Measures

Measure	Definition
Clients (Users)	
Visits per capita	Count of the total number of people who enter the library each year divided by the population served
Visits per hour	Count of the total number of people who enter the library each year divided by the total number of hours the library is open each year
Percent of population with items on loan	Total number of individuals with items on loan divided by the service area population
The Budget	
Expenditure per client (user)	Total budget divided by the total number of clients (users)
Expenditure per borrower	Total budget divided by the total number of clients (users) who borrow materials
Expenditure per circulation loan	Total budget divided by the total number of circulations (annually)
Expenditure per reference transaction	Total budget divided by the total number of reference transactions (annually)
Expenditure per open library hour	Total budget divided by the total number of hours the library is open annually
Cost per visit	Total budget divided by total number of visits to the library (gate count)
Cost per capita	Total budget divided by total population of the community

Measure	Definition
Collection	
Circulation	Number of items charged out annually. Includes initial charge outs and renewals. Includes items from the general collection and reserves
	Circulation data are often broken down into type of materials loaned, subject categories, and so forth.
In-library materials use	Number of items used in the library but not charged out.
Total materials use	The sum of circulation and in-library materials use.
Circulation per capita or circulation/1,000 population	Total circulation divided by population served
In-library materials use per capita	Number of items used in the library but not charged out divided by population served
Total materials use per capita	The sum of circulation and in-library materials use divided by population served
Average number of items borrowed per user	Total circulation divided by number of users who borrowed materials
Circulation per staff	Total circulation divided by total number of staff (FTE)
Circulation by material type	Count of materials borrowed separated by type of material (by branch)
	Material type includes adult fiction and nonfiction, children's fiction and nonfiction, videos and DVDs, audiocassettes, etc.
Circulation by borrower type	Count of materials borrowed sorted by borrower type (by branch)
	Borrower type includes adult, children, seniors, residents, nonresidents, etc.
Circulation by geographic location	Count of materials borrowed sorted by geographic location (address) of borrower
	In some cases, data can be exported to a GIS system and maps created.

Measure	Definition
Circulation per public services staff	Total circulation divided by total number of public services staff (FTE)
Circulation per hour open	Total circulation divided by total number of hours the library is open
Circulation (loans) per visit	Average number of items borrowed per client visit
Loans per registered client	Total circulation divided by total number of registered clients
Proportion of borrowers as a percent of total service area population	Total number of borrowers (in the last year) divided by the total population, expressed as a percentage
Collection turnover: average circulation per volume	Total circulation divided by total number of volumes in the collection
Proportion of circulating collection on loan	Count of the number of volumes on loan divided by the total number of volumes in the collection, expressed as a percentage
Circulation of new monographs	Count of the number of titles borrowed at least once during the past year compared to the total number of titles added to the collection during the last year—expressed as a percentage
Proportion of collection borrowed	Count of the number of volumes borrowed at least once during the year divided by the total number of volumes in the circulating collection, expressed as a percentage
Proportion of collection unused	Count of the number of volumes not borrowed (borrowed + in-library use) during the year divided by the total number of volumes in the circulating collection, expressed as a percentage
Proportion of collection borrowed, by subject categories	Count of the number of volumes borrowed at least once during the year, sorted by subject categories, divided by the total number of volumes in the circulating collection, sorted by subject categories, expressed as a percentage

Measure	Definition
Holds (reserves) per copies held	Count of the number of holds (reserves) divided by the total number of copies (volumes) in the library's collection
Percent of holds satisfied in two weeks, four weeks	Number of holds satisfied within two (or four) weeks divided by the total number of holds placed
Materials availability, sometimes called measurement of availability	Proportion of materials sought by a library client at the time of their visit available for use (on the shelf), typically expressed as a percent
Materials owned by the library	The probability that the materials sought by a client are owned by the library
Items borrowed and never returned (as a percent of circulation)	Count of the number of items borrowed from the library and never returned divided by the total annual circulation, expressed as a percentage
Items borrowed and never returned (as a percent of size of collection)	Count of the number of items borrowed from the library and never returned divided by the total size of the collection, expressed as a percentage
Citation information correct	The probability that the client will bring complete and/or accurate citation information
Client's skill at the catalog	The probability that the client is able to locate an item in the library's catalog which is owned by the library
Material on the shelf, sometimes called shelf occupancy rate	The probability that the item sought by the client is not checked out
Material availability: on the shelf	The probability that the desired item is to be found at its correct location on the shelf
Client location skills	The likelihood that the client is able to locate the item located on the shelf
Requested materials delay	Time users must wait for the desired material, normally expressed in days

Measure	Definition
Amount of intra-system movement of materials	Count of the number of items moved from one (branch) library to another to fulfill the request of a client
Intra-system materials delay	Time users must wait for the desired material, normally expressed in days
Workload per staff member	Total circulation divided by total staff (FTE)
Overdues per circulation	Count of the number of items overdue divided by annual circulation
Turnaround time for shelving books	Count of the number of hours (days) it takes to place an item on the shelf after it has been returned to the library
Technical Services	
Number of titles ordered	Count of the number of titles ordered
Number of items ordered	Count of the number of items ordered
Number of purchase orders placed	Count of the number of purchase orders placed
Number of titles received	Count of the number of titles received
Number of items received	Count of the number of items received
Number of materials cataloged	Count of the number of items cataloged
Number of journal issues received	Count of the number of journal issues received
Number of journals routed	Count of the number of journals routed
Reference Services	
Number of reference transactions	A reference transaction is an information contact that involves the knowledge, use, recommendation, interpretation, or instruction of one or more information resources between a library client and a library staff member. Typically directional questions are not counted. Libraries will sometimes sort by those reference transactions that take less than 10 minutes and those transactions that take more than 10 minutes.

Measure	Definition
Number of reference transactions	Total number of reference transactions divided by the service area population
Proportion of correctly answered reference transactions	"Test" reference questions are provided to volunteer clients. The clients ask the question and record several things about the reference process, including the answer. The provided answer is then compared to the "correct" answer and the percent correctly answered is calculated.
Number of virtual reference transactions	Annual count of the number of reference transactions received and responded to electronically: e-mail, Web form, chat (and in the future, videoconferencing)
Reference transactions per circulation	Total number of annual reference transactions divided by total circulation
Document Delivery	
Number of documents ordered	Count of the number of documents ordered
Document delivery fill rate	Proportion of the number of documents received compared to the number of documents ordered, expressed as a percentage
Speed of document delivery	Time from when a document order is placed until the document is received, expressed in number of days (hours)
Cost of document delivery	Total of the charges incurred to order documents using a document delivery service

Would include any annual minimum subscription charge plus the per transaction charges. |
| Turnaround time for photocopies | Time from when a photocopy request is placed until the photocopy is received by the client, expressed in number of days (hours) |

Measure	Definition
Interlibrary Loan (ILL)	
Number of items requested	Count of the number of items requested from another library
ILL fill rate	Proportion of the number of items received compared to the number of items requested, expressed as a percentage
Speed of ILL	Time from when an item request is placed until the item is received, expressed in number of days (hours)
ILL fees	Fees charged by other libraries to loan a item to another library
Requests received from other libraries	Count of the number of requests received from another library
ILL requests as a proportion of total circulation	Count of the number of items requested from another library divided by total circulation
ILL photocopies	Number of photocopy pages produced to meet client ILL needs
Information Alerting	
Number of current information alerts (sometimes called selective dissemination of information or SDI)	Count of the number of current information alerts sent to clients (alerts may be sent using e-mail or snail mail)
Number of current information alert users	Count of the number of current information alert users
Library Information System	
Number of staff hours spent servicing information technology in public service areas	Total number of staff hours (information technology staff, professional librarian, paraprofessional, clerical, and volunteers) spent in service information technology in public service areas (typically data gathered during a one-week sample period)

Measure	Definition
Online Catalog	
Number of online catalog search sessions	Count of the total number of user search sessions
Number of online catalog searches	Count of the number of online catalog searches, often sorted by types of searches.
Number of successful online catalog searches	Count of the number of online catalog searches that retrieve some records but retrieves fewer than some number (generally less than 100 records).
Number of items/records examined	Count of the number of full-text articles/pages, abstracts, and citations viewed In some cases, these statistics are sorted into text only and text/graphics viewed.
Public Access Internet Workstations	
Number of public access Internet users	Count of the total number of users of all of the library's Internet workstations (typically the count is done using a one-week sample)
Average annual use rate of Internet workstations	Count of the number of hours the library-owned Internet workstations are busy divided by the number of library owned Internet workstations times the number of hours the library is open, usually expressed as a percentage
Number of Internet workstation hours available per capita	Count of the number of hours the library Internet workstations are available for use divided by the total service area population

Measure	Definition
Databases	
Number of database sessions	Total count of the number of sessions (logins) initiated to the online databases Some libraries track sessions initiated from within the library, outside sessions, and total sessions.
Number of sessions per capita	Total count of the number of sessions initiated to the online databases divided by the total service area population
Number of database queries/searches	Count of the number of searches conducted in the online databases Subsequent actions by the user, for example, sorting and printing, are not counted.
Number of items/records examined	Count of the number of full-text articles/pages, abstracts, and citations viewed In some cases, these statistics are sorted into text only and text/graphics viewed.
Cost per session	Cost of licensing the electronic database(s) divided by the total number of sessions
Cost per document (record) viewed	Cost of licensing the electronic database(s) divided by the total number of documents (records) viewed
Percent rejected sessions	Number of times a user attempts to connect to the library's electronic resources and is unable to do so (library's Internet connection, server or software is down) divided by the total number of successful and unsuccessful sessions

Measure	Definition
Virtual Visits	
Number of virtual visits to networked library resources	Count of visits to the library via the Internet (and dial-in access, if provided): visits to the library's Web site, the library's online catalog, and access to online databases
Facilities and Library Use	
Attendance	Number of user visits to the library
Activity attendance	Total number of individuals who attend a specific activity, e.g., children's story hours, film or lecture series, etc.
Activity attendance per capita	Total number of individuals who attend a specific activity divided by the service area population
Remote uses	Number of library clients who visit the library's Web site and online catalog remotely
Total uses of the library	The sum of attendance and remote uses
Library visits per capita: public library measure	Attendance divided by the population served
Program attendance	Count of the number of people who attend various programs annually
Program attendance per capita	Count of the number of people who attend various programs annually divided by the population served
Program attendance per staff hour	Count of the number of people who attend various programs annually divided by the total number of staff hours involved with planning and presenting programs

Measure	Definition
Facilities use rate	Proportion of time, on average, that a facility is being used
	All kinds of uses are included: user seating, workstations, photocopy machines, reference services, use of the collection, and so forth.
Service point use	Average number of users at a public service point, for example, reference, circulation, or information desks
Building use	Average number of people in the library at any one time
Use of library equipment	Count of the number of hour's library equipment is used, for example, microform machines, photocopiers, and so forth
Number of photocopies produced	Count of the number of photocopies produced
Seat occupancy rate	Count of the number of seats (chairs) being used compared to the total number of seats
Instruction	
Client information technology instruction	Total number of clients instructed and total number of client instruction hours
Staff information technology instruction	Total number of staff instructed and total number of staff instruction hours
Out-of-Library Services	
Number of persons served	Count of the number of persons served by the outreach programs, for example, delivering library materials to the home bound, senior citizen clubs, book deposits, and so forth
Bookmobile circulation	Count of the number of items loaned via the bookmobile

Measure	Definition
People served by the bookmobile	Count of the number of people who use the bookmobile service
Number of bookmobile stops	Count of the number of bookmobile stops

Satisfaction-Based Output Measures

Measure	Definition
General satisfaction	Users report their satisfaction levels, typically using a written survey, during this library visit on specific library services and their overall satisfaction with the library.
Reference satisfaction	Users evaluate the reference experience and their overall satisfaction with reference services.
Online search evaluation	Users evaluate the performance of the search intermediary and the search results and give indication of their overall satisfaction with the online search service.

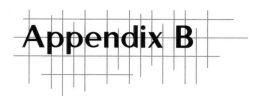

Appendix B

Toolbox of Performance Measures and Indicators*

A. The Library Context

MEASURES

Population	Target population
Cost/financial data	Gross current expenditure
	Net current expenditure
	Income generated
	Capital expenditure

INDICATORS

Costs: Population	Net current expenditure per capita
	Capital expenditure per capita

B. Staff

MEASURES

Costs	Expenditure on staff
	Expenditure on staff by main function

INDICATORS

Costs: Population	Total expenditure on staff per capita
	Expenditure on professional staff per capita

C. Service Points/Opening Hours

MEASURES

Provision	Number of service points
	Service point hours open
	Weighted average hours open per week
	Floor area occupied by library services
	Total library floor area

INDICATORS

---

* Adapted from Suzanne Ward, John Sumsion, David Fuegi, and Ian Bloor. *Libraries in the Information Society: Library Performance Indicators and Library Management Tools.* Luxembourg: European Commission, 1995.

215

Provision: Population   Library floor area per capita

D. Library Users

MEASURES
Use   Number of registered library members
                         Number of active library users
                         Number of active borrowers
                         Users by category (type of patron)

INDICATORS
Use: Population   Active library users per capita
                         Active borrowers per capita
                         Analysis by demographic and other features
                              of active library users and active borrowers

E. Library Uses

MEASURES
Use   Library visits
                         Remote uses of the library
                         Program/activity attendances

INDICATORS
Use: Population   Library visits per capita
                         Remote uses of the library per capita
                         Program/activity attendances per capita

F. Library Materials

MEASURES
Cost   Materials expenditures
                         Price indexes
                         Expenditures on binding/conservation
Provision   Number of items added to collection
                         Number of titles added to collection
                         Current periodical titles received
                         Number of books on order
                         Updated reading lists
                         Number of items in the collection
Use   Number of loans

Number of issues from closed access
Number of items on loan
Items not borrowed over a period of time
Items borrowed over a period of time
Number of titles on loan
Number of holds on titles
In-library use

INDICATORS

Costs: Population	Materials expenditure per capita
Costs: Costs	Expenditure on binding/conservation per capita
	Materials expenditure per capita – historically
Provision: Population	Number of items added to collection per capita
	Number of titles added to collection per capita
	Copies added per title added
	Items in collection per capita
	Age of items in collection
Use: Population	In-library use per capita
	Loans per capita
	Titles loaned per capita
	Items on loan per capita
Use: Provision	Issues per item in collection (turnover)
	In-library use per item in collection
	Proportion of items on loan
Needs filled	Proportion of reading list material provided
	Needs fill rate
	Expert checklists
	Mis-shelving rate
Timeliness	Speed of acquisitions and processing
	Speed of delivery from closed access
	Overall speed in satisfying "requests"
	Speed of obtaining recalled/reserved items
	Speed in satisfying requests for material at another site or service point
Satisfaction	Users' satisfaction with library stock

G. Inquiry Services

MEASURES

Use	Number of information visits
	Number of reference transactions

INDICATORS

Use: Population	Reference transactions per capita
Satisfaction	Reference satisfaction survey
Needs filled	Information success rate
	Proportion of queries satisfied in an unobtrusive test

H. Interlibrary Loans

MEASURES

Cost	External cost of interlibrary loans service
Use	ILL requests made of other libraries
	ILL received from other libraries
	ILL items sent to other libraries

INDICATORS

Timeliness	Time taken to satisfy ILL requests
Use: Use	Proportion of ILL loans to total loans
Use: Population	ULL per capita

I. Library Facilities

MEASURES

Provision	Number of readers' seats in the library
	Number of items of equipment in the library (OPAC workstations, personal computers, photocopiers, microfilm viewers, etc.)
Use	Proportion of time equipment is in use

INDICATORS

Provision: Population	Number of users per reader seat provided
	Number of items of equipment in the library per capita
	Seat occupancy
	Facilities use rate
Satisfaction	Users' satisfaction with library facilities
	Services used

Appendix C

Quality-Oriented Performance Indicators*

General Library Use
Market penetration
Opening hours compared to demand

Collection Quality
Expert checklists
Collection use
Subject collection use
Documents not found

Catalog Quality
Known-item search
Subject search

Availability of Documents
Acquisition speed
Book processing speed
Availability
Document delivery time
Interlibrary loan speed

Reference Service
Correct answer fill rate

Remote Use
Remote use per capita

User Satisfaction
User satisfaction
User satisfaction with services offered for remote use

---

* Adapted from Roswitha Poll and Peter te Boekhorst, Eds. *Measuring Quality: International Guidelines for Performance Measurement in Academic Libraries.* IFLA Publications 76. London: K. G. Saur, 1996.

Appendix D

Key Performance Indicators*

Objective	Recommended Performance Indicator
Provide appropriate infra-structure capacity to meet the needs of the community	❑ Square feet of public access floor space/square feet per capita ❑ Total visits ❑ Total circulation ❑ Hours per branch per spare feet ❑ Customer survey
Provide an appropriate level of materials provision/investment	❑ Total cost of materials (acquisitions budget) ❑ Number of items/titles purchased annually ❑ Market segment match to materials purchased (acquisitions budget) ❑ Acquisitions budget per capita ❑ Market segment "fit" for total collection (materials targeting) ❑ Age of materials
Optimize efficiency and effectiveness of staff resources	❑ Total public access staff (fulltime equivalent) ❑ Total public access staff hours ❑ Total activity index / public access staff hours ❑ Total public access staff expenditure ❑ Customer survey

*From MicroPlan and PractiCo Pty. Ltd. Victoria Public Libraries: Key Performance Indicators. Melbourne, Australia, Local Government Branch, Department of Infrastructure, 1999.

221

Objective	Recommended Performance Indicator
Provide product quality (material, program, or access) in terms of market focus	❏ Market segments by age and ethnicity ❏ Percent of collection to each market segment ❏ Community wide survey ❏ Customer satisfaction survey
Direct financial resources efficiently and effectively	❏ Total budget ❏ Total budget per capita ❏ Total budget per public access sq feet/hour ❏ Total budget per total activity index
Optimize information technology	❏ Number of public access computers (terminals) ❏ Number of public access computers per capita ❏ Total number of hours public access computers / (total number of hours library open times number of public access computers) ❏ Number of electronic "hits" ❏ Customer survey
Maximize number of customers	❏ Total active customers ❏ Market segments ❏ Total active customers as a percent of population ❏ Compare active customers with total activity index ❏ Customer survey
Provide a comprehensive policy framework to deliver effective service to meet community needs	❏ Are the plans and policies linked to the overall goals of the library service and local government ❏ Are the plans and policies relevant, up-to-date, reviewed frequently and reflect demographic change ❏ Are there a range of relevant and up-to-date strategies in place, e.g., information technology, human resources, collection development

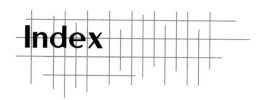

Index

About the Author

JOSEPH R. MATTHEWS is an internationally renowned on library automation and information systems, and president of his consulting company, Matthews and Associates, Carlsbad, California.